mirror mirror

by Kara Powell and Kendall Payne

Reflections on who you are *and* who you'll become

ZONDERVAN

Mirror, Mirror: Reflections on Who You Are and Who You'll Become

Copyright © 2003 by Youth Specialties. Youth Specialties Books, 300 South Pierce Street, El Cajon, CA 92020 are published by Zondervan, 5300 Patterson Avenue SE, Grand Rapids, MI 49530.

Library of Congress Cataloging-in-Publication Data

Powell, Kara Eckmann, 1970-
   Mirror, mirror : reflections on who you are and who you'll become / by
Kara Powell and Kendall Payne.
            p. cm.
Summary: Offers information and advice, with personal anecdotes, on what girls think of them-selves and why, emphasizing a faith-based perspective on self-image.
   ISBN 0-310-24886-8 (pbk.)
   1. Teenage girls--Religious life--Juvenile literature. 2. Teenage
girls--Conduct of life--Juvenile literature. 3. Self-esteem in
adolescence--Religious aspects--Christianity--Juvenile literature. [1.
Teenage girls--Conduct of life. 2. Self-esteem--Religious
aspects--Christianity. 3. Christian life.]   I. Payne, Kendall. II.
Title.
   BV4551.3.P69 2003
   248.8'33--dc21
                                                              2003006649

Unless otherwise indicated, all Scripture quotations are taken from the Holy Bible: New International Version (North American Edition). Copyright © 1973, 1978, 1984 by International Bible Society. Used by permission of Zondervan Publishing House.

Web site addresses listed in this book were current at the time of publication. Please contact Youth Specialties via e-mail (YS@YouthSpecialties.com) to report URLs that are no longer operational and replacement URLs if available.

Edited by Rick Marschall and Jim Kochenburger
Cover and interior design by Electricurrent www.electricurrent.co
Proofreading by Anita Palmer
Printed in the United States of America

05 06 07 / DC / 10 9 8 7 6 5

mirror mirror

by Kara Powell and Kendall Payne

Inside... mirror mirror

"Every day...is a walking Miss America contest."
(Reviving Ophelia, p. 55)

* Introduction by KARA POWELL

If that's true, where do you stand? Are you on the stage as one of the finalists? Maybe even the one who will be crowned with her own sparkly tiara? Or perhaps you are one of the 45 contestants who got cut WAY early in the contest. Or maybe you never even made it into the contest. You're sitting in the audience—outside you're applauding but inside you're envying the "perfect" beauties parading across the red carpet in front of you.

Who do you feel like: Miss America or Miss Piggy?

If you're like us, it's some of both. Some days we don't even like to look in the mirror. Other days we think we look OK. And on those rare days, we may even think we look pretty good. We are our own harshest judges.

Maybe that's because we've been doing it for years. Lots of years. If every day is a walking Miss America contest, we've had decades of competition. And scoring. And failing.

If you looked at us on the outside, we look pretty successful. Kara's got her Ph.D. (that means she's a doctor—that also means she went through 26 grades of school). Plus she's got a great job, an awesome husband, and two of the cutest kids around. Kendall's a gifted musician with a recording contract who gets to travel extensively doing what she loves to do. Good stuff, all.

But if the camera zooms a little closer, you'll see we've got some warts. Lots of them. And they've been growing for years. Neither one of us did a very good job keeping diaries or journals, but if we could go back to when we were your age, here's what I, for instance. might say.

Kara's Story...When I was 12

When I was 12, I was boyish. I was one of those tomboy types. I was tall (still am), had short hair, wasn't allowed to get my ears pierced, and wore hardly any make-up. When I went to restaurants, waitresses would often think I was a boy. I pretended that it didn't bug me. I kinda' liked being a tomboy. But I wish it didn't happen so often. I wish there was more about me that looked and acted like a girl.

And I was eager. The most popular girl at our junior high school was named Kim. She was my friend's friend's friend, which meant she probably knew my name, but nothing else about me. I knew lots of stuff about her – what radio station she listened to, who she was going out with, where she shopped, what she did for fun. Every once in a while when we'd walk past each other in the hallways, she'd say, "Hey." That meant THE WORLD to me. She saw that I existed. And that made me feel a little more important.

Plus I was ashamed. Junior high meant Junior high P.E. And junior high P.E. meant changing in the junior high girls locker room. For the first year of junior high, I could wear whatever I wanted for P.E. Sometimes I didn't even change. Especially not my shirt. I'd wear the same shirt to class and to P.E., even in the winter when I didn't sweat too much. But in eighth grade we got a junior high dress code. I had to wear a white shirt with this dorky roadrunner on the pocket (that was our mascot — really threatening to other teams, I know). That really stunk. That meant I had to change twice — right before and right after P.E. I'd put my back to the rest of the room, which felt like the rest of the world, and changed as quickly as I could.

Lots of stuff was new. Especially stuff about boys. I remember the first boy who asked me to dance at a junior high dance. He was Italian and cute—one of those dark and handsome types. In high school, he became a drug dealer and dropped out of school, but in junior high, he was cool. I remember what I was wearing. And I remember how I wore my hair. But what I remember most of all was that my hands were sweaty. Like dripping. (What's funny is that even as I type this now, my hands start to sweat.) I wanted Joey to like me. He liked me enough to dance. Once. We never really talked after that.

I always felt on the outside. I remember hearing about friends' birthday parties and thinking, "Why didn't they invite me?" After all, I had invited them to my birthday party. But I guess I was closer to them than they were to me.

When I was 16...

My brother was the cute one in our family. Blonde hair. Blue eyes. Tan. He always had a girlfriend. Girls who didn't even know him would stop and flirt with him.

I was the smart one. If you need a math problem solved, give me a call. I had school pretty well wrapped. If there was one thing I was good at, it was tests.

How I wanted to feel pretty. To feel cute. To have strange boys flirt with me like girls flirted with my brother. But that hardly ever happened.

Plus I was the friend of the pretty one. One of my best friends in high school was our Homecoming Queen senior year. I, ahem…drove the car that she rode in during the parade.

Someone once did some math and figured that if a Barbie doll was a real life woman, she'd be 7'2" tall and have 40-22-36 measurements. Her neck would be twice as long as a normal woman's. That's a far cry from the 5'4," size 12, 37-29-40 average woman who lives here in America.

Walt Mueller, "*What You See Is What I Am*," Youth Culture Today, Spring 2001, 1

Two of my other best friends were cheerleaders. And you know what that means—instant cuteness. Don't mind me—I'm the tall, awkward one standing next to the popular, bubbly cheerleaders.

And I was the convenient one. From 7:30 am-2:10 pm Monday to Friday, my life revolved around my school. From 4 to 6 every afternoon, my life revolved around the pool and swim team. The pool and the school were about two blocks apart and my house was smack dab in the middle. That meant lots of people came over to my house—during lunch, after school, to get a snack, to borrow a towel. Instant popularity. But I had to wonder, was it really me, or was it just that they didn't feel like going all the way back to their own houses?

Continued on next page...

When I were 22...

At least I look better now. My hair is way longer and I highlight it. I spend more time and money on my clothes. I even wear this year's styles instead of last year's. I actually see guys turning their heads to check me out. And not just dorky guys. Cool ones too. I'm no beauty queen, but I'm way better than before.

Plus I'm dating more. Well, at least lots of first and second dates. The relationships don't seem to last very long.

But I'm also comparing more. I've been comparing myself to other girls as long as I can remember. But I've gotten meaner about it. I gained some weight in college, and I remember seeing a friend from high school who had also gained the freshman fifteen pounds. I thought to myself, "Thank goodness I'm not the only one."

Speaking of food, I'm definitely into calorie counting. When I was in high school, I could eat whatever I wanted, and thanks to two hours each day of swim team, it never stuck to me. But I've gotten older and my metabolism is slowing down. 800 calories in a piece of pizza. 525 in a beef taco. 437 in a scoop of ice cream. I've got it all memorized, and what I don't know, I look up later when I go home—-just to see if I should feel guilty about what I've eaten for dinner or not.

And I've got a new fear. My dad and mom got divorced when I was six years old. My mom always made it seem like my dad left her, which in many ways is true. But I'm realizing that I was in the house too. When he moved two miles away into his own apartment, he moved away from me too.

It's not like I blame myself, but I sometimes wonder if whatever it was that caused him to leave is going to cause other men to leave me. Maybe all men. Maybe I'm just destined to be abandoned.

Well, now you've got an idea where we're coming from—flaws, fears, crises of confidence, bad-mirror days and all. Our hope is that these pages will encourage you and reassure you. Together we will loosen the grip on us from the fear-feeding "Mirror, mirror on the wall, who's the fairest of them all ..." philosophy. We will explore a godly path to freedom. Here's what's in store for you as you turn these pages:

✳ *A book of stories.* We've talked to girls and women all over the country (plus a few guys — at least the ones who don't have cooties) about how they feel about themselves. What they like about themselves, and what makes them cringe. Sometimes they've written their own stories. Sometimes we've done it for them.

✳ *Your story.* As you read other people's stories, we hope that you recognize paragraphs and pages out of your own story. In fact, we've prayed for that. And we've left room for you to jot down some thoughts, take quizzes, and ask yourself some hard questions. This isn't a book you're reading for your History class. It's a book you're reading to help you in LIFE. So chew on it. Digest it. And then see what happens.

✳ *True story.* In every chapter, we talk about our favorite true story: the story of God's love for us messed-up people. We don't always understand why God loves us. In fact, we hardly ever do. But we're glad he does. And we want you to be glad too.

"Mirror, mirror on the wall"
is not the last word on any of us, at all. You'll see.

Kara Powell

Editor's note: MIRROR, MIRROR is a book that we have designed as a magazine, to encourage you to pick it up and put it down, to read long and short articles, to respond to different moods and flavors... as you would with your favorite magazine. Light stuff, heavy stuff: it's all here, just like life. Kara, veteran youth leader and teacher, has written most of the text. Kendall, rising star of Christian music, has written some signed reflections in each section. The rest of the pieces have been written by a hundred girls like you. Check it out... read some cool stuff... and reflect!

mirror mirror

by Kara Powell and Kendall Payne

Make-Up

* **LIPSTICK**
  * **COLD TURKEY**
  * **ADDICTION**
  * **AND A QUEEN?**
  and these are related how?

* **Plus:** Test your own Make-Up I.Q.

Lipstick

Blush I can handle. Eye shadow I dig. Eye liner is easy. Mascara is simple.

But lipstick. Lipstick is a different story.

I've never liked it. In high school, friends would subtly hint, "Hey Kara, wanna try my lipstick?" Or they'd be not-so-subtle, "Kara, you really need to wear some lipstick. You'd look way better."

So I'd try. I'd lean toward the mirror and make that really stiff smile you're supposed to make when you put on lipstick, and give it my best shot. But invariably, it'd end up smeared. Or it would look so bright that I'd blot it off. I'm the kind of girl who wants lipstick that looks like you're not wearing any. In my opinion, they should make that a whole brand. It could be called lipstick-that-looks-like-natural-but-you're-still-wearing-something lipstick.

I can't even buy lipstick by myself. I have to bring a friend. I have a friend who is like in love with lipstick. Lipstick is her thing. She wears it all the time, and it always looks great on her. I asked her for some advice once. She dug in her purse through her seventeen lipstick tubes and handed me one. "Bronze Beauty" it was called. On me, it looked like Majestic Mud.

So last night I went to Macy's with my husband to buy some lipstick. While he's not savvy enough to tell the difference between Natural Nude and Rosy Nude, I knew that he wouldn't let me buy anything too horrendous.

There were two women behind the counter. One was wearing about a half-inch of foundation. When she smiled, I thought her face would crack. Seriously.

The other woman looked more normal. More like me. I went to her.

She sat me down and gave me one of those so-that's-what-I-really-look-like mirrors. First we started with lip liner. I leaned in close to the mirror and really concentrated on what I was doing, and it actually turned out OK. Then we went for the lipstick. Barely Blush was a bit too light. Natural Wonder was better. Wanting to risk a bit, I scanned the lipstick towers myself. Usually I only try on lipsticks that have the word "Barely" or "Natural" or "Nude" in them, but I figured I'd go wild and crazy and try Pink Pleasure. Yikes. Way too pinky. Even my husband kinda grimaced.

After a few more bronzy, orangey, and maroony samples, I decided that the second one I tried, Natural Wonder, was the best. I bought it and the lip liner and went on my merry way to the food court.

What's interesting is that I walked out of Macy's feeling better about myself than when I walked in. I'm 31 years old. I spend all sorts of time helping girls see that they don't need make-up to feel better about themselves. And yet my $21 purchase gave me a lift. I could take on the world knowing my lips would be up to the job.

Is that bad, OK, or even good? What does it say about me that two items that weigh about 2 ounces make me feel so much prettier?

These are tough questions to answer. But in this chapter, we're going to try. As you read the articles, we invite you to think about your own make-up issues. Do you feel like you need it? Do you feel naked without it? Do you feel worse about yourself without it? Why wear it in the first place?

And you'll probably think of even better questions. So read on.

Make-Up...a Tax Deduction for Me

By Kendall

Make-up is a tax deduction for me. Whatever I buy, that I only wear on stage, is a write-off. What that means (for those of you who don't pay taxes yet) is that at the end of the year I figure out how much money I've made and I pay taxes on that. But there is such a thing called deductions.

Which means if I made $100 I'd owe them $20 of it. But if out of that hundred dollars I spent $50 of it doing something related or involving my career then I only pay $10 dollars. Make sense? (Excited about doing your taxes?)

I do have a point. The profession I am in wants me to look as beautiful as possible. I can't tell you how many times I've been at a concert. And when I sit outside at the table where I sign autographs a little girl or little boy comes up and picks up my CD. They hold it about arms length away from them and then look at me. They squint their eyes and look back and forth from the album cover to my real face a couple of times and then they say it. "Is this really you?" I'm like, "NO! I'm selling someone else's album! Duh!" What are they implying, I ask myself. Do I really look that different?

The Photo Shoot

My record company spent $20,000 dollars on my photo shoot—which could buy me a brand new car. Now it wasn't all on air brushing and stuff like that. It was renting the place and booking the photographer, hair stylist, make-up artist, and clothing designer. (And for all the food. It was really, really good food. Which I tried very hard not to eat...unsuccessfully.)

Three hours before the shoot, my hair is blown out perfectly straight (which I can never seem to do on my own). I've got concealer under my eyes with the consistency of fudge frosting. I'm getting sweaty and so someone has to stand right beside me with a blotting towel and more powder. I've got clothes on that cost so much I just burst out into laughter when I see the tag (tags still attached...on loan and headed back to the store that night).

There is soft artificial lighting in addition to the natural sunlight to give me just the right glow. There is music being played to make me "happy." I am also wearing the tallest boots in the world with long pants because it's an optical illusion... in other words they make me look thinner. It was great fun while it lasted!

Back to Reality

The reality is, at about 10 that night I changed into the clothes I came in, which, I think was like a t-shirt and jeans. I got into my dirty pick-up truck and drove home. I washed my face with some generic brand of soap and laughed at what the washcloth looked like. I crawled into bed and realized I'm not any different.

About two weeks later I got to go into a room and look at all the pictures. There were hundreds and hundreds of them. It was surreal. I couldn't believe this girl was me. I knew that I didn't look like that. And yet here I was deciding what face I was going to show the world. Makeup does wonders...and it's a tax write-off for me!

I grew up in a Vineyard church. And Vineyards are somewhat known for great worship. This one was no exception. Every Sunday and Friday night, I could be found somewhere in the auditorium face down and probably crying. God showed up and I went down.

Continued on next page...

Captive Heart

Music captured my heart at a young age, especially in worship. As life went on I realized that I also had a talent to write songs, not just sing. And so I began to write about my struggles and joys and about super-models. It worked! Someone thought it was decent material and gave me a record deal! But the desire to worship was still there, it never left and probably never will leave.

When you tour so much there are many things you learn about being on stage. I've picked up little tips and tricks to help me have better shows. It always helps if you feel attractive walking out there, so here are my little things to do:

First of all, black eyeliner. It makes my eyes stand out like nothing else, so that's a must. Next, foundation and powder (which I never wear in normal life), all over my cheeks. Because of my red hair and fair complexion, when I overheat, my face looks like a hot house tomato! So pile that foundation on, baby! When my hair was short, I would always try to pull it off my forehead because my sweat makes my hair curl, and of course it is the age-old dilemma—if your hair is straight then you want it curly and vice versa. Also it doesn't matter if your clothes are comfortable... as long as they look good.

Make-up Doesn't Worship Well

On the final night of a long tour, I decided to play my favorite worship song at the end of my set. It was one of the most moving experiences I've ever participated in and I learned a lesson I'll never forget.

As I stood up there with all my make-up on I realized that no one in the audience was looking at me, they all had their eyes shut. No one out there cared if my mascara was rolling down my face with my sweat and tears. No one was looking at me...their hearts were focused on the one they were worshiping. More important than all of them not looking at me, God himself was looking at me. And he saw through not only the make-up on my face, but the clothes on my back, and the skin on my bones. He saw all the way into my heart. And only he, not anyone else in that room, could see if I was beautiful or not.

And so that is why I've decided that make-up doesn't worship well. It runs, it goops and most importantly it takes my focus off him and puts it back on me. Isn't it funny how we rush to the bathroom and touch ourselves up because we live in a physical world. God inhabits a spiritual world. We think *In Style* magazine defines beauty? I think God himself is Beauty. The more we look like him the more truly beautiful we will become. There's food for thought.

I do wear makeup

So I just got home from a show back East and I thought that the story was all too fitting not to share with you all. I had an early flight. And when I say early I mean 6:45 a.m.! Which means be there at 5:45, which means wake up at 4:30. So what is the normal clothing attire for someone who flies that early? Tennis shoes and baseball caps I tell you! And as comfy of clothes as you can find, if you can even make it out of your pajamas!

I arrive without a speck of makeup on. Not even lip gloss (which I always think means I've at least tried to look put together). The person who came to pick me up was a young, attractive gentleman. When you travel as much as I do and get picked up by strangers every time you fly in, you begin to recognize who's looking for you before they realize it's you. So this guy looked at me and I could tell he entertained the possibility, but then decided, "naaaaaaa. It can't be her. Kendall Payne is a rock star. And that girl couldn't be a rock star if she tried."

*make-up

By Julia

The key to having your make-up look great is by using it as a tool to accent the natural beauty that God has already blessed you with. God created each of you uniquely and beautifully. Everyone has different skin types and tones, eye colors and face shapes. Accept and appreciate what is beautiful about yourself, and then have fun playing up your features.

The other key to having your make-up look nice is to first take care of your complexion. If you don't maintain healthy skin, what's the sense in trying to enhance it with color, right?

So here are some tips towards healthier skin:

* Drink plenty of water each day.

* Get enough sleep at night.

* Use good skin care products that are designed for your skin type, morning and night. They should include a cleanser, a toner, a mask and a moisturizer.

* Follow up with sunscreen which protects and seals in all of that good care.

* Keep your hair and hands off of your face as much as possible. They can transfer dirt and oils, causing blocked pores and blemishes.

* Speaking of blemishes, try not to squeeze pimples. Squeezing them causes scarring and spreads more bacteria to the surrounding area. Continue to clean the area as normal and use a mild acne product if necessary.

* Be careful of strong acne cleansers that sting; they can actually dry out and irritate the skin, damaging it more.

Think of applying make-up as art, and that your face is the canvas, and well, your brushes are your brushes! A good artist will paint her entire canvas all the same color before she begins to paint in order to create a smooth and even surface, and so the colors stand out even better in contrast. You can do the same with your face by using foundation.

Foundation not only helps defend your face from harmful elements like UV rays from the sun or impurities in the air, it also evens out the skin tones of the face and helps cover blemishes. If needed, apply concealer before foundation in order to cover larger blemishes or to minimize darkness under the eyes.

Some tips on choosing and using the right foundation:

* Be sure to select a color that matches your skin tone. It should almost disappear into your skin.

* Do not use foundation to try to change your skin color or tone. It should cover lightly and look natural.

* Always try on a foundation before you purchase it. Your hand is not a good test area. Actually sample it on your face, and in natural lighting.

* A good way to find the right match is to test three shades at the same time.

* Apply small stripes of each shade on your cheek, one above the other.

* Whichever one disappears is the best. If in doubt, ask your mom or a friend to help you decide.

* Foundation can either be applied with your fingertips or a sponge, using light upward motions.

* Be sure to cover your whole face, but you do not need to pile on a thick layer. Again, think natural.

* Take the time to blend it in well, especially along the jawbone and hair line to avoid a noticeable line of color.

*Cold Turkey

I started wearing make-up when I was eleven. Some of my friends got to wear it when they were ten. But my mom's always behind the other moms, so I had to wait a whole extra year.

It was just lipstick at first. And really, it was more like lip gloss. Then blush and mascara. By high school, I was into eye shadow, foundation, the works. I wore make-up every day to school, but I didn't wear as much as my friends did. They wore like twice as much as me. So I felt like it was still OK.

In college, I moved into a dorm where guys lived on the same floor as me. One side of the hallway was men, the other side was women. Lots of the women didn't wear any make-up. Lots wore lots of make-up. I was somewhere in the middle. As usual.

It's interesting to live with guys on your floor. Actually, that's an understatement. It's zany, embarrassing, and exhilarating. No matter what time of day or night, when I walked down to the bathroom down the hall, or went down a few rooms to visit a room, I ran into a guy. Sometimes we'd just say, "Hey." Other times we'd chat a bit about the next calculus test, and sometimes I'd end up in full-blown conversations about intramural football.

So I wanted to be wearing make-up. Even more than that, I needed make-up. Don't get me wrong: if it was 2 a.m. and I woke up to go to the bathroom, I wouldn't plop on some lipstick or mascara. But from the time I woke up until the last minute possible before I went to bed, I kept my make-up on. Sometimes before dinner, I'd freshen up my lipstick, eyeliner, and mascara. If I worked out, I'd shower and redo my make-up.

And on those rare occasions when I wasn't wearing make-up (like 2 a.m. bathroom runs), I'd walk looking down at the ground. I didn't want to look up and make eye contact with anyone. It felt like if I didn't really see them, they wouldn't see my plain face.

I didn't think much of it, but one day my roommate said to me as I was putting on some blush for dinner, "Do you realize that you never go anywhere without make-up?" Huh.

I let her question sink in. She was right. I had become the thing that I had tried to avoid in high school: I had become make-up dependent.

When you become dependent on something, you've got a few options:

1. Keep on doing what you're doing and try not to worry about it.

2. Do it a little less.

3. Stop cold turkey. Don't do it anymore.

I went for option 3. No make-up from January to spring break. Three months of just my face without any special pinks, browns, teals, or greys. Just me.

At first it was weird. Really weird. For one

Continued on next page...

thing, I spent less time in front of the mirror. But even more than that, I got more comfortable with how I looked. Not overnight. It took lots of nights, about 43 to be exact, for me to stop looking down when someone walked toward me. For me to stop thinking as I sat at dinner, "I'm sitting with Kyle and Tyson and I'm not wearing any make-up." For me to stop envying the other women on the floor who still got to wear it.

And I gave in a few times. That eyeliner and mascara was just a little too tempting when Sunday Flicks rolled around. But of the 92 days between January and spring break, I only caved 7 times. Not bad.

When spring break rolled around, I busted out my make-up bag. And I put on all my old colors. But even though I put on the same amount of everything, it felt different. I didn't need it. I wanted it, but I didn't need it.

After I finish typing this, I'm going to go get ready for class. And that means not just putting on jeans and a T-shirt, it also means putting on my powders and pastes. But they don't control me anymore.

Think about it...

* Do you think you have control over make-up, or does make-up control you? Why?

* Would you go cold turkey and not wear make-up for a few weeks? Why?

* What does your answer above tell you about how important make-up is to you?

* What one thing will you do to make sure that make-up does not control you?

Test Your Make-Up I.Q.

Sure, you know how to match your lipstick with what you're wearing, and what kind of mascara works best when you dive into the pool, but let's see how much you know about how it all began, and what it's like now. Do this: Choose your response, True or False, to each of the following statements.

1. *True False:* **The earliest historical record of cosmetics comes from 2920 B.C.**

2. *True False:* **A few thousand years ago, men and women in Egypt used cosmetics equally.**

3. *True False:* **The women of Egypt used soot from fires to blacken their eyelashes.**

4. *True False:* **In the first century A.D., the Romans used chalk to whiten their faces.**

5. *True False:* **It's likely that the Jews of the Old Testament learned about cosmetics from the Egyptians.**

6. *True False:* **Many deodorants today contain aluminum sulfate, which closes the openings of the sweat glands.**

7. *True False:* **Americans spend about $10 billion on cosmetics per year.**

8. *True False:* **The majority of cosmetics are purchased in department stores.**

9. *True False:* **Perfume is a type of cosmetics.**

10. *True False:* **Estee Lauder is the most popular brand of cosmetics in department stores.**

Answers:
1. True 2. False – women used cosmetics more than men. 3. True 4. True 5. True 6. True 7. False – it's actually around $14.5 billion 8. False – department store purchases account for a little less than $5 billion. 9. False – it's considered separate from cosmetics. 10. True

No-Nonsense
Nail Care

Your hands are appendages or extensions of the largest organ on your whole body: your skin. Beautiful, strong fingernails are generally a sign of good health and good habits.

Massage cuticles with a good thick moisturizer or vitamin E before bedtime. Hydration is very important because 72% of our skin is composed of water. Drinking water and applying moisturizers is very beneficial.

Never cut your cuticles. The cuticle band is there for an important reason – to protect the nail matrix and root to allow for healthy nail growth. If your cuticles seem a bit aggressive, the best way to train them is to gently rub them back in a circular motion with the towel after you wash your hands. Carefully trim the occasional large, loose piece of skin around the nail. Remember, the moisturizing will help.

Keep the edges sealed by smoothing them with a fine nail board. File in one direction only. Your fingernail is constructed of overlapping layers. Avoid sawing back and forth, as this opens up the layers and causes them to chip and peel. Clip excess length off before filing.

Apply a nail strengthener if nails tend to be weak or peeling. Take special care to cover the very edge of the nail.

Keep nails at an active length with the free edge no longer than 1/3 of the nail bed length. This keeps your hands looking good and available for whatever activities you are involved in. Natural and clear polish is always chic. Dark colors and the French manicure look best on the active length nail.

Be careful not to misuse them. Fingernails serve as protection for the fingertip and assist in grasping, but are best not used as tools.

Steer clear of artificial nails. Harsh chemicals are used in these products. They cause temporary damage to your nails that can take 6 to 12 months to grow out. Another cause for concern is that the chemicals used are absorbed through your skin into your body. Natural is always better than artificial.

✳ Why I LIKE Make-Up

I didn't wear very much make-up in high school. I was too busy to worry about that stuff. I always just thought make-up was fun, unless you wore it so thick you would need a putty knife to slap it on.

Then I went off to college and was surrounded by the "natural" or "hippy" types of people. Women didn't wear make-up there (they also didn't shave, but that's a story for an entirely different kind of article). So those around me encouraged me not to wear make-up. It was actually a very freeing time. No muss, no fuss, roll outta bed and go!

I can remember being a counselor for a Jr. High Summer Camp during one of my breaks during college. All of the Jr. High girls in my cabin brought these huge "Caboodles" with them full of make-up and hair products. Caboodles are basically these huge, pink plastic boxes with all sorts of compartments to hold all of your beauty-care products (go in the garage and look at your parents' tool or fishing tackle box and you will get the idea). I was amazed. The head counselor peeked her head in and it took her a while to figure out I was the counselor.

"Over here," I said, "I'm the one without the make-up on!"

Sold on Make-Up, Or Am I?

It wasn't until I started teaching that I really got into wearing make-up. I wanted to look professional. I didn't want to look like one of my Jr. High students. My friend was working at Nordstrom. There was this new brand of make-up she wanted me to try. One of the make-up artists gave me a makeover, and I was hooked. There are now stores that ONLY sell make-up…. Shelves and shelves of it! It makes me happy to go into those stores. I find make-up fun and artistic. I enjoy the new season trends.

The question is: Is that sinful? Can I enjoy something so seemingly worldly? Can I enjoy something that appears closely tied to vanity? What are my motives for wanting to wear makeup? These and more are all very good questions for me to ask about anything in my life. I am not so sure the answers are easy or clear-cut.

What about other hobbies or art forms? What about someone who practices the piano for hours and hours a day? At what point is desiring excellence bordering on vanity? What about my friend who designs websites? Can he spend hours and hours doing that? Is that considered a worldly pursuit?

I have a friend who used to wear make-up every day and felt she did not look pretty without it. Her self-esteem was tied up in her morning rituals of make-up and hair primping. A few years ago, she felt convicted to not wear make-up anymore. She only wears lipstick now. God brought her to a place of letting go of that dependency in her life.

To each her own?

I think that is such an awesome example of how God works. Our Heavenly Father sees us as individuals. He convicts us of our sin in personal ways.

I have another friend who doesn't wear make-up because she seems to think that men don't like it. Is that a pure spiritual motive? Is she more godly because she has cast away all of the superficiality of make-up?

Personally, I enjoy make-up for its creative elements. I put make-up on my friends some times for special occasions. I love to share it with others. I enjoy going shopping with friends and helping them with new make-up.

My Struggle…Make-Up and Beyond

OK Let's bring this back to my neighborhood. To understand me, you've got to know that I struggle with my body image. I struggle with my weight. I think one reason I like make-up is that I don't have to be a certain size to fit into a lipstick. Yet I still wonder, Is make-up sinful? Sometimes.

Can I enjoy something so worldly? Define worldly.

Is make-up bringing me closer to vanity? Maybe.

Is it a sin? If we define sin as something that separates us from our personal relationship with Jesus, we realize that sin isn't just our actions. Sin is more about the parts of ourselves that others can't see: our motives, our thoughts, our feelings and our desires.

So, yes, I have found myself becoming too dependent on make-up. I actually made a covenant with my small group that they would hold me accountable to my spending habits, especially when it comes to buying the latest make-up. I have shared with them my insecurities and fears, because the root of the problem is my struggling self-esteem.

The painful question I often ask myself is: Will any guy find me attractive? I am single and at an age where most of my friends are married with children. They have husbands who tell them they are beautiful. Somehow make-

Continued on next page…

up gives me at least some control over the way I look and present myself to others. However, if I am truly honest with myself, then I need to remember that God is in control of that area of my life. He hasn't made a mistake with me. He has me exactly where he wants me.

When Make-Up Use Turns Sinful

Make-up is a sinful part of my life when I use it to give myself worth or value. Like when I rely on it to make or break how my entire day will be, and unfortunately sometimes that is truer of me than I would like to admit. I can't forget that the qualities that I possess inside are far more valuable than anything on the outside.

When make-up seems to bring me such happiness, I need to stop and ask myself why that is. Sometimes I go on a make-up "fast" where I basically go without make-up for a day or two (and not just on a day when I won't see anyone!). I find on those days I check myself less often in the mirror and realize that my day was just as wonderful.

Think about it...

* When does make-up use become a bad thing...or sinful? Why?

* Why do you use make-up (IF you do)? How are your reasons the same or different from why other girls wear make-up? Explain.

* What's the biggest problem with make-up use? The greatest positive reason for using it?

* Can you still be beautiful without make-up? Why?

* Can you still be happy without wearing make-up? Why?

Test Your Hair I.Q.

True or False...

1. Brushing your hair 100 strokes a night=healthy hair.

2. As long as someone says a certain hairstyle or hair product is OK, it is.

3. Good-looking hair is available for all hair types.

4. Being happy with your hair is expensive.

5. You should do what you want because it's your hair.

1. **False.** Brushing your hair too much can increase breaking of ends. For some types of curly hair, you shouldn't use a brush at all. A wide-toothed comb would be better.

2. **False.** Sometimes the latest trend or fashion doesn't look as good on you as it might on others. Make sure you find the best style for you.

3. **True.** You might wish you had straight hair instead of curls, or vice versa, but generally, you can find a hair style that is popular and perfect for your hair.

4. **False.** Ask your hair stylist for products that are inexpensive and effective. They might give you some great ideas.

5. **False.** It might be "your" hair, but it's not worth fighting with your parents or doing something drastic to your hair just to make a statement. Ask others for advice, and when they get it, listen carefully.

Here Comes the Queen

There go the pretty people. Five girls and five guys making their way up to the stage. Time for Homecoming Court. Whoopee.

I go to a Christian high school, so they try to squeeze in the Bible wherever possible. Before crowning the king and queen, our principal reads 1 Peter 3:3-4, "Your beauty should not come from outward adornment, such as braided hair and the wearing of gold jewelry and fine clothes. Instead, it should be that of your inner self, the unfading beauty of a gentle and quiet spirit, which is of great worth in God's sight."

Yeah, right. What planet is he on?

He actually said that this wasn't a popularity contest, and it wasn't about who was the best looking on the outside. (Your planet again?) It was about inner beauty, he said.

If that's true, then why are all five girls skinny? And why do they all have acne-free skin and great bodies? Why were they the most popular girls?

Inner beauty. Hah. Try outward appearance, plain and simple.

And the rest of us sit and watch. And clap. And smile on the outside. But inside, we're not feeling so beautiful. We're the mediocre masses watching the fabulous, perfect, popular few.

When Peter wrote about inner beauty, he was actually talking about wives. The most gorgeous wives were those who didn't rely on external props, but rather worked on who they were on the inside. Instead of paint, shadow, and polish, they put on humility, gentleness, and kindness.

So does that mean that Peter thought that women should wear no make-up? Go au naturale?

Probably not. The key was the woman's focus.

I like to think of it like cake. Cake by itself is yummy. But if you add a little bit of icing, a thin layer that's not too sweet, the cake tastes even better. Too much icing can drown out the cake and make you gag.

The same is true with make-up. Every person is beautiful already. But if you want to wear make-up to accent your sparkling eyes and great smile, that's OK. Just don't put too much on. It drowns out the real you.

Think about it...

* Have you ever felt like this writer as you've watched the "pretty people?" Why?

* Which words, or phrases, from 1 Peter 3:3-4 stand out to you? Why?

* Would you say your use of make-up is "frosting on the cake" or more? Why?

* What are your favorite features to enhance with make-up? To cover up?

* Read 1 Peter 3:3-4 (above) again. How does this passage challenge your views of make-up use? How will you respond to this in your own life?

Are You Addicted?

Are you wondering if you're a little too dependent on make-up? Are you addicted to it, or can you handle a day without it?

Do this: Take the following quiz, circling every statement that describes you.

I own more make-up than can fit in a brown lunch bag.

I carry around at least five kinds of lipstick.

When I meet a girl, I often think about how she would look better if she wore more blush or different eye shadow.

I spend more than seven minutes per day doing my make-up.

I spend more than $20 per month buying make-up.

I touch up my make-up during school (lipstick doesn't count!).

I do my make-up even before a quick errand outside the home.

I'd skip a day of school instead of going to school without make-up.

I avoid kids from school if I'm out running errands and not wearing make-up.

I stay out of the swimming pool because of what it will do to my make-up.

I pretty much always keep a mirror with me.

Reality check: If you circled more than six of the eleven statements above, you might be addicted to make-up.

Think about it...

* *Do you think you're addicted to make-up?*

* *How would your mom or step-mom answer that question? Your best friend?*

* *How did you feel as you took the quiz?*

* *What scares you, if anything, about going without make-up? Wearing make-up?*

* *What do you think God would say about those fears?*

*Real Guys

Don't you wish you could get into a guy's mind and really figure out what he's thinking? Us too. So we did the next best thing: we sat down with a bunch of guys and asked them questions. Deep questions (well, you know, relatively deep). Provocative questions. The kinds of questions that you wish you could ask them yourself.

They came up with pretty diverse answers. Maybe that's because they are a pretty diverse group of guys:

Chris J. is 14 years old. He spends most of his time playing football, basketball and video games. Oh, and cracking jokes.

Kevin C. is a 17 year-old senior. He's tall, so he plays volleyball, and in his free time, jams on his guitar.

Drew W. is a 16 year-old who's way into sports. He plays basketball and is his high school quarterback. As a sophomore, that's pretty impressive.

Edmund J. (E.J.) likes sports like the rest of them, but this high school junior also likes mixing it up in paintball. He's quieter than the rest, but when he talks, he's got good stuff to say.

Fifteen year-old *Jonathan M.* is a sophomore who is into sports, but also "digs movies and girls." (His words.)

Michael K. is a 14 year-old freshman who's into his computer, video games, and golf. Not putt-putt golf. We're talking the real thing.

And last is 17 year-old *Brandon W.* He likes to dabble in everything from computers to music to water polo. A real Renaissance man.

So you'll be hearing from these guys throughout the book in articles we'll call "Guys Do Deep." Don't worry. They don't bite. They just talk about the truth as they see it.

Make-up. Lots of times we wear it because we want to look good for guys, but do they really like it? Do they like the Cover Girl® look, or would they rather have us go natural? We asked our real guys:

How much make-up should a girl wear?

E.J. Y.: "Just a little, so it's not really noticeable."

Drew W.: "Just a tiny bit."

Chris J.: "I think a girl shouldn't wear any make-up. She should show her natural beauty."

Brandon W.: "It's OK to wear some make-up, but not so much that you can't see what she looks like without it. She shouldn't have to feel like she always needs it."

Jonathan M.: "Not a lot. Maybe a little eye shadow or lipstick, but not a whole lot."

Michael K.: "Not so much that you cover your face. Just a touch up."

Kevin C.: "Not too much. Just enough for a little color, but no changing of skin color."

mirror mirror

by Kara Powell and Kendall Payne

BOYS, BOYS, BOYS

* **BOY CRAZY**
A Roller Coaster Ride

* **HOW NEEDY ARE YOU?**
How do You Rank?

* **DATING NON-CHRISTIANS**
Some Reasons for Both Sides of the Debate

* **Plus:** What do you think of Dear Abby's advice?

*Boys, Boys, Boys

The Guy Zone...Enter With Caution

"I love you." There are no three little words more magical, powerful, and potentially life-altering than these.

As girls, we want to be loved. To hear those three words. We need to be loved, and to give love in return (so do guys, they're just not as clued in as we are). And so we look everywhere for it.

Our parents...Our sibling...Our friends...And guys...

That last one is a tricky one. We have a legitimate, God-ordained thirst for relational intimacy. And every day that we don't like who we are, it's like a teaspoon of salt gets poured down our throats.

Every day that we look at the mirror and say, "Yuck," we get a little more salty. And a little more thirsty.

Every day that we curse our bodies and wish we were someone else, that healthy thirst becomes a bit more desperate, a bit more eager, a bit more willing to be satisfied by the first thing that comes along. That usually means the next guy who walks our way.

And some weeks something different happens. Every day we wish we could look like someone else, our throat gets a little smaller. A little less able to swallow, a little less likely to drink. So we stay away from guys. We can't handle them. We don't like ourselves, so why should a guy like us, much less love us?

Our struggles with self-image take the wonderful gift of guy-girl relationships and complicates them. Kind of spoils the fun a bit. Makes us act way differently than we really are. Adds all kinds of pressure. At least lots of days it ends up that way.

But not every day.

Some days we feel OK, or maybe even good, about ourselves. We greet guys like friends, like brothers, like dates. We don't run away and we don't rush in. We walk calmly, patiently, confidently.

Our hope is that by now in this book, you like what you see in the mirror, at least a little bit more than when you started reading. And that maybe you don't need a boyfriend to feel good about yourself. You just need yourself, and your God, to feel good about yourself.

But it's not always easy. We're older than you; one of us is even married with a kid, and we still deal with these same questions. Maybe the articles in this chapter will set us all on the path toward some answers.

Getting Noticed

By Kendall

At the tender age of 16 I was nobody's girlfriend. But I wanted to be.

I was completely preoccupied with guys. And I knew somehow that they were definitely not preoccupied with me. I didn't know what to do. My best friend was really into makeup and so she tried to help me, but it wasn't totally successful. And as for my fashion sense, well let's just say that I wore all things baggy.

There was a cool skater store in the mall by my high school. I had to go there one day after school. Upon entering the store I realized I had walked into boy heaven! There were about six adorable guys all standing at the counter just talking. My first thought was, "Ok, pretend like you don't notice them. Now, flip your hair and glance over your shoulder." (I at least knew that much.)

I turned to find something that wounded me deeply. NONE of them were looking. I just didn't understand. Why didn't guys like me? But then something amazing happened to me. I felt like God said, "Kendall, there are millions of guys in this world. Some will think you're attractive, and some won't. But ultimately there is only one man in this entire world who you have to attract and that will be your husband."

I walked out of there free as a bird. Free to not let those boys make me feel unattractive because they didn't look at me. It's hard to believe when you're in high school and junior high—and quite honestly, even when you're a single adult.

We all want to be found attractive, but in the end, there is only one man you will spend the rest of your life with. And so who cares what all these other guys think about you?

So the real question comes down to this. What are you doing to the woman on the inside of you that will attract the kind of man who won't settle for superficial beauty?

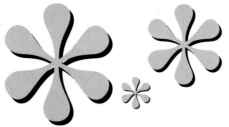

N is for Nivia
(Who's Never Had a Date)

I haven't dated much. OK, that's an understatement. I haven't dated at all. I'm in eleventh grade, and I've never been asked out. Unless you count the Sadie Hawkins dance last year, but I'm the one who did the asking. So I guess technically I went on a "date," but I don't really count it.

I just don't know how to act around guys. Like, take flirting. Some girls are so good at it. They know how to stand, how to toss their hair, how to say, "Hi there," in such a seductive way. I just stand there like a blob.

Sometimes I don't even stand there. Sometimes I run away from a guy I like. It's my act-aloof-and-like-you-don't-need-him strategy.

Last week I tried it at Geoff and John's party. I like Jeff (not the one throwing the party, a different one). Jeff was standing near the back door, so I went with Krista and we stood near enough so that he could see us, but far enough so that it wasn't like we were trying to be seen. I acted like I could care less about Jeff. Like I didn't even know he was there. But every few minutes I turned my head just enough so that I could see him out of the corner of my eye, hoping to see him looking over at me. No luck.

It's not that guys never like me. Every few months I hear about one who does. But I just don't know what to do to show them I like them back. So usually I just avoid them.

H is for Hannah
(Who's Never Been Hurt)

What is it with me? Why do I keep going out with guys a few times and then breaking up with them?

Take Jeremy, for example. He is soooo cool. On our first date, he took me for a picnic at the park. For our second date, we went and saw a movie and then had hot chocolate for dessert. For our third date, he surprised me and took me to the spring carnival.

But on the way back from the carnival, something inside me just snapped. I got scared. Jeremy was so great. I liked him so much. So what if he decided he didn't like me anymore? What if he saw who I really am and realized I'm not good enough for him? He's too good to be true, and soon, he was going to realize it.

So once we got to my house, Jeremy asked me what was up. He said I had seemed distracted on our drive home. I told him I didn't want to go out with him anymore. It's not that I didn't like him. It's just that I was scared.

And it's not like I want Jeremy to promise he'll always be with me. We've only gone out on three dates. If he said he'd never leave me, I wouldn't believe him.

With Josh, I lasted six dates. Billy was my all-time record at fourteen dates. I liked him more than anyone else I've ever gone out with, which was why we made it all the way to fourteen. But it's also why I had to break up with him. If he abandoned me, it would hurt too much. Or more like, when he abandoned me, it would hurt too much. I had to end it first.

A is for Alana
(Who Always Has a Date)

I can't remember the last time I haven't had a boyfriend, or at least been pretty close to having one. Guys just like me. It's not like I'm drop dead gorgeous or anything. I just give off this vibe.

It's a good thing, too, because I always feel better when I have a boyfriend—both about myself and life overall. There's just something so comforting about having a guy who takes care of me, who I can call if I'm upset about something, who takes me out on fun Saturday night dates.

Jimmy is the best boyfriend I've ever had. He is way better than Erik, my last one. Erik was so busy with his job and with wrestling that we hardly ever saw each other. But Jimmy's got plenty of time for me. Don't get me wrong: he's got his own life and stuff. But if I need him, he's there for me. I don't know what I would do without him.

The Bridal Shower

By Kendall

Most girls spend all their "single years" wishing for a husband. I am pretty confident to use the word "most" because it is a rare find when a woman honestly says she is perfectly content in her singleness. And even then I rarely believe them, unless she's a nun.

One of my favorite television shows is called "A Wedding Story" on TLC. In one half-hour I am invited to celebrate with a couple I've never met before on the greatest day of their lives. I'm pretty much a sucker when it comes to the sentimental stuff. I cry nine times out of ten. Unfortunately it's on right at lunchtime. So if you can imagine me weeping over my tuna fish sandwich, too embarrassed to answer the phone, afraid that someone will ask me why I'm crying and I'll have to explain. But I love it!

A couple of months ago I received an invitation to a bridal shower for a good friend of mine. After the gifts were opened, and punch consumed, all the women gathered around the bride-to-be to offer some words of wisdom. Some women were cheesy and said things like, "As long as you two really love each other everything will be all right."

I was like, "Oh pa-leeease! She needs a little bit better advice than that!" This marriage thing is tough stuff, I at least know that and I'm not even in one yet! After a few more of these comments I was so bored I was about to slip out the back door. Luckily just then a woman said something that perked my attention. She said, "Well honey, now that you're getting married, it is crucial that you find yourself some good girl friends."

I thought, now that's weird. She's marrying the man of her dreams, he is her best friend, the one she wants to spend every day with for the rest of her life, and yet you're telling her the most important thing is to hang out with girlfriends? The bride herself looked as perplexed as I felt so I knew there was an explanation to follow.

This wise woman began to explain that many a bride expects her new husband to fulfill all of her needs. She has been dreaming about this since she was a little girl and now every memory of prince charming and the words "happily ever after" come flooding back to her subconscious. She has longed for the day when "the two shall become one" and plans on taking it literally. "But it is at this moment," she said, "above all else you, must guard and protect your individuality."

My face twisted into a very confused snarl. I'd never heard these thoughts before and more importantly I didn't know if I wanted to hear them now. Sensing, I'm sure, the crushing blow she just served to each young woman's fantasy, she continued.

Quoting Kahlil Gibran (I had to ask her to write these words on a napkin after the shower was over because it impacted me so powerfully) she said,

"Sing and dance together and be joyous,
But let each one of you be alone.
Even as the strings of a lute are alone
Though they quiver with the same music.
Stand together yet not too near together
For the pillars of the temple stand apart
And the oak tree and the cypress
Grow not in each other's shadow."

What this means, she explained, is that the miracle of marriage is not when a person marries another person and the two become one, that's just math! The miracle happens when one whole person chooses to love honor and cherish another (entirely separate) whole person, and then two whole people become one.

She said to the bride, "You cannot grow in your husband's shadow or you will die. A tree needs its own sunlight, its own water, its own ground to spread its roots wide and deep. It cannot share any of these things with another tree, no matter how much they love each other, if it wants to stay alive. Your independence is not a sign of weakness, but of strength. Your distance from each other will be the very thing that draws you close. It's like Rilke says [who I later found out was a poet] 'love consists in this, that two solitudes protect and border and salute each other.'"

"I told you to find some girl friends so that your identity does not become wrapped up in being his wife. So that you can bring something into this marriage not just dissolve into it like a lump of sugar in coffee."

I was shocked, to say the least. Maybe other women knew this truth inherently but it came as a news flash for me. It finally made sense; you don't lose yourself in marriage, you gain another whole self. I had spent years of dating pouring myself into the relationships, wondering why I felt so empty at the end. Always concluding that "he" just wasn't the right guy. Now I realized I was never meant to give my sense of self to anyone else.

The next few minutes were a blur. I was so deep in thought I didn't realize everyone was standing up gathering their purses and coats. I left that bridal shower feeling more equipped for marriage than I had ever been. "All that's left now," I thought to myself as I drove away, "is to find a boyfriend and get engaged!"

Think about it...

* What did Kendall mean by not giving "her sense of self" to anyone else in dating?

* How do "guard and maintain your individuality" while dating?"

* Who is the boy of your "dreams"? Describe him.

* How did this article affect your view of guys and dating?

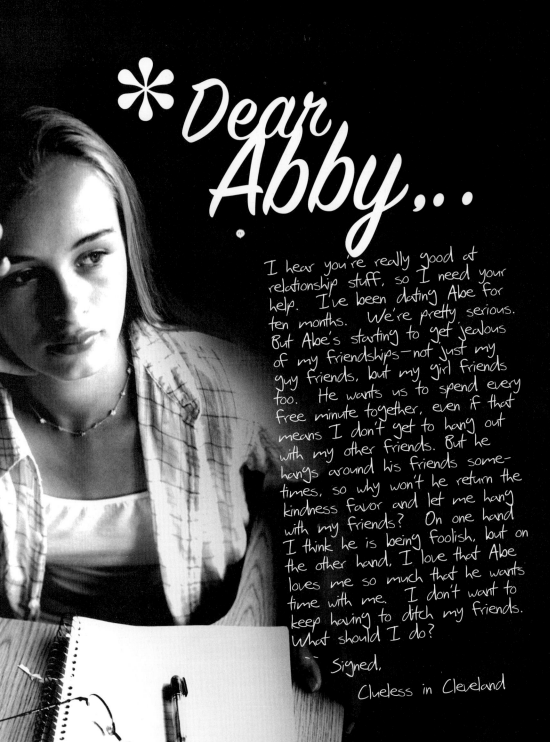

*Dear Abby...

I hear you're really good at relationship stuff, so I need your help. I've been dating Abe for ten months. We're pretty serious. But Abe's starting to get jealous of my friendships—not just my guy friends, but my girl friends too. He wants us to spend every free minute together, even if that means I don't get to hang out with my other friends. But he hangs around his friends sometimes, so why won't he return the kindness favor and let me hang with my friends? On one hand I think he is being foolish, but on the other hand, I love that Abe loves me so much that he wants time with me. I don't want to keep having to ditch my friends. What should I do?

-- Signed,

Clueless in Cleveland

Dear Clueless,

You've got yourself a common problem. You're right to wonder if Abe's demands on your time are right, especially when they take you away from your friends. Your life, though filled with him, has many other people in it. It's right for you to want to spend time with those people.

I think you should do the right thing, regardless of what your boyfriend wants. If he's truly a good guy, and if he really cares about you, he wouldn't expect you to ditch your friends. If he cares, he would want you to be happy. You're happy hanging with your friends so he should encourage that.

And if he's not such a good guy, who doesn't really care about you, who expects your whole life to revolve around him, he's not worth your time. I've seen guys like this even get jealous of their girlfriend's relationship with God!

There are lots of other fish in the sea, and you've already got a puny anchovy on your hook. My advice…go fish!

Signed,

Abby

Think about it...

* What do you think of Abby's advice? Agree/ disagree? Why?

* What do you think of the advice to "go fish"?

* Why do you think girls sometimes are willing to do something they know is wrong for a guy? What might they be afraid of?

Abby has learned the hard way that you have to do the right thing, even if the guy closest to you wants you to do something different. Her full name is Abigail, and she lived 3,000 years ago. She was married to Nabal, whose name meant "Fool." (That's not a good sign. Would you want to hang out with a guy who was named Stupid or Lamebrain?)

Abby lived around 1000 B.C., but then, like now, women had to constantly figure out how to respond to men's wishes.

It turns out that King David, and his men had helped Nabal by protecting his men and sheep. In 1 Samuel 25, King David later heard that Nabal was "sheep shearing," which was something you did when you were getting ready for a big party (did they know how to have fun, or what?).

David thought this would be a good time for Nabal to thank him and repay him for his protection by giving them some food. Nabal, a self-centered man, showed great disrespect to David, even claiming not to know who King David was.

David had been wronged. He gathered 400 of his soldiers and was packing up to kill Nabal and all his men. But just as he was riding over to Nabal's house, Abby met him. Abby had heard what Nabal had done, and since she knew that wasn't right, she offered David lots of food (grain, raisins, and pressed figs—once again, did those folks know how to have fun, or what?).

David accepted her offer, and because of Abby's courage, he decided not to kill Nabal. That was a good thing: both for Nabal, and for David, who didn't need to make any more blunders as king.

In a strange twist, Nabal died anyway. When Abby told him what she did, and when he realized how close he came to dying, his heart failed him and he had a stroke. He died ten days later, and David ended up asking Abby to marry him.

Imagine if Abby had done nothing. Not only would her husband have been murdered, but she would have let God's king make a mistake. She had courage. She had guts. She was willing to go against what her man wanted because she knew it was wrong.

Think about it...

* When has a boyfriend tried to get you to do something wrong?

* How did you respond?

* How would you handle it differently if it happened now?

* It is said that right emotions follow right actions—your desire to do what is right grows as you continually practice right things. In what one area of your life—especially involving boyfriends—do you need to practice right actions right now?

Do the right things, even if you don't feel like it and want to do what's wrong much more. Your desires will get purer and right over time.

Boy Crazy

By Betsy

In junior high and high school, I was definitely boy crazy. There was always at least one boy's name that I would doodle anywhere and everywhere there was space on my notebooks... sometimes there were a few names. The names often changed, but not the game. I would set my sights on "the man of my dreams" and measure my self worth by his response. If he showed interest, then I felt great about myself—no interest, then I knew there was something wrong with me.

The worst was when it wasn't quite clear. Then my sense of value went up and down like a roller coaster.

The beginning of my boy craziness was just the names, the crushes and the doodling. None of those boys even knew (I don't think) who I was or that I was so "in love" with them. I still cringe when I watch an old home video from Christmas in seventh grade where I run up to the camera yelling "I love Chip!" I don't recall having a single conversation with Chip, but apparently something about him caught my fancy.

There was also Josh whose locker received many of my anonymous notes. I do recall a few of my conversations with Josh. They were "hiii...." And I thought to myself, "I can't believe I'm passing him in the hallway" (even though I memorized where he was at each moment of each passing period). Yep, I was pretty boy crazy.

8th grade "payoff"

Then came 8th grade. Boys started paying attention to me. My first boyfriend lasted all of one day. As we stood outside of my first period science class, he said those amazing words, words I had only dreamt of before... "Will you go with me?" I was in disbelief – I had a boyfriend! I think we ignored each other for most of the rest of the day.

He came to youth group that night, along with some other guy friends of mine... and the truth of my boy craziness emerged. As we hung out that night I realized I liked too many of these boys, so therefore having ONE boyfriend didn't make sense. Thus, the one day relationship ended. However, that day made me feel pretty good – after all some guy liked me!

The self worth game

What had developed out of my daydreaming, doodling boy craziness was a game of some sort. This game to me was a challenge. (Mind you I was not clearly thinking of this during the time—during the time I was just thinking "ooooh .... he's cute!")

What was won or lost in this challenge was my self esteem,

self worth, sense of value—whatever you want to call it—but basically how I felt about myself. When I was dating or being pursued by a guy I targeted, I felt pretty good about myself... at first. The more I got involved in this game, the more my self worth depended on it.

Once I started dating someone, my self worth was often based on the way he treated me. As we all know, as nice as guys are, they aren't perfect. So, if my boyfriend wanted to go out with his friends, rather than me, I began to think I wasn't very important. Much of who I saw myself to be was wrapped up in what guys thought of me... they were my measuring stick.

Well, needless to say, finding my self worth in my relationship with guys was a rocky road. Many seasons in life I felt I was not an attractive person, inside or out. If guys didn't pay attention to me, then I didn't think I was very important.

Not only does it hurt to not feel important, but it can be very lonely. I think we as humans are designed to desire to be loved, cared for and wanted. Unfortunately, I chose to meet those desires only in my relationships with guys. When guys were interested it was great, but when they weren't it hurt deeply.

In junior high I think I began to realize these desires to be loved, cared for and wanted. Unfortunately I set a pattern of looking to guys to meet those needs.

To this day, as a happily married wife and mom, I still struggle in looking in the right place to truly have these desires met. No matter how great a guy is (and my husband is amazing!), there is no guy that can perfectly fill those desires. I am still learning to look to God to find perfect love. Only He can consistently and completely love me, care for me and communicate that I am wanted by him.

How Needy Are You?

Do this: Read each situation below. After each situation you will find three possible responses A, B, and C. Rank these responses by writing one of the following number before each letter:

3= most likely response,

2= second most likely response, and

1= next to your least likely response.

Story 1:

You've been eyeing Kevin for a while. He just moved to your town from Danville, and man, is he cute. Your friends think he's cute too, but since you're the one who has computer class with him, you're the only one of your friends who knows him. At lunch, Kevin looks around the cafeteria for someplace to sit. You know he doesn't know many people, and that he doesn't have many friends, so you...

    A. Look away. You wouldn't want him to think you were watching him or anything.

    B. Run up to him, offering to take his tray as you escort him to your table.

    C. Casually wave and gesture to your table as your mouth the words, "Wanna sit with us?"

Story 2:

It's your first date with Samir. You've been friends ever since your calculus teacher changed the seating chart and moved him next to you. As you open your closet, you pick out...

    A. Jeans and a T-shirt. Wouldn't want to look too eager, or like you had dressed up for him or something.

    B. A strapless dress. You've seen guys eye you when you've worn it before, and you want to get Samir's attention. This ain't math class, after all.

    C. Black pants and a sweater. Nicer than what you normally wear to school, but not too nice.

Story 3:

Marco breaks up with you because he says he's not ready for a serious girlfriend. But soon you hear he's dating Lynda. After three weeks, she dumps him. A week later, your phone rings. "It's Marco. I really miss you, and I want to get back together with you." You say...

    A. "You've got to be kidding me." After all, you don't want to get hurt again.

    B. "Can we go out tomorrow night?"

    C. "I'll have to think about it. I'll get back to you in a few days."

Story 4:

All your friends are talking about the boys they like. They ask you who you like. You secretly like Chad, but you haven't told any of them. You say...

- A. "No one. You know me."

- B. "Are you kidding? Chad is the cutest guy at the school. I sooooo like him." And secretly you hope someone will tell Chad.

- C. "Well, I haven't told anybody yet, so please keep it confidential. I think I like Chad."

Now transfer your scores into the following chart and add up the total points you got for As, Bs, and Cs.

Story 1 A_____ B_____ C_____
Story 2 A_____ B_____ C_____
Story 3 A_____ B_____ C_____
Story 4 A_____ B_____ C_____
Totals: _____ _____ _____

Which letter had the highest point total?

If it's A, you're probably a bit afraid.
. Maybe you've been hurt in the past by your dad, step-dad, brother, or someone you were dating. Maybe you haven't had much experience dating. Either way, you tend to hide from guys, and you should probably work on that a bit. You might want to try being a bit more friendly, or just a bit more like yourself, when you hang out with them. Ask a friend if she has any advice for you about how you can be more yourself when you're with them.

If it's B, you're probably a bit eager.
Guys are important to you, maybe a little too important. You might have dated quite a bit, or maybe your eagerness scares guys off. Either way, there's something in you that feels like you need a guy, so you dive in pretty quickly. Try moving a little slower toward guys and find hobbies other than boys. Not only will this make you a better person, but it will eventually make you a better person to date.

If it's C, you're fairly balanced.
And that's good news. You relate to guys, but don't cling to them. Keep that up, and ask a friend to warn you if you start to either get too distant or dive in too quickly. Since balance is often something we swing through on our way to another extreme, don't assume that you can stay balanced without a lot of help from God and friends.

Is It OK to Date a Non-Christian?

We know that lots of you reading this book are Christians. And you've maybe heard at your church or youth group that you shouldn't date someone who isn't a Christian. Why do you think that might be?

We interviewed two girls, both of whom are followers of Jesus:

Jenny thinks it's OK to date non-Christians. Here are some of her reasons:

* Non-Christian guys act the same, or sometimes even better, than Christian guys.

* I have the chance to convert them when I date them.

* There are more non-Christian guys than Christian guys so they're easier to find.

* There are no guys at my church who I would want to date.

* There are some decent guys at my church, but I've known them so long that they are more like brothers than boyfriends.

Pam thinks that Christians should only date Christians. Here's why:

* Paul writes in 2 Corinthians 6:14 that Christians shouldn't be "yoked" with non-Christians.

* Non-Christian guys are more likely to want to go farther sexually.

* Even though I'm only a teenager, I could fall in love with a non-Christian guy and then want to marry him. It happens, you know!

* My parents won't let me.

* Christian guys are less likely to try to challenge my values, dragging me to parties and movies that I really don't want to go to.

Think about it...

* Read Jenny's and Pam's lists again. Put a check mark next to anything you've thought before. Circle any of their points that you currently believe.

* Which list has more checks—Jenny's or Pam's?

* Which list has more circles—Jenny's or Pam's? Why do you think that is?

* Is it okay for a Christian to date a non-Christian? Why?

* Five years from now, do you think your answer will be different?

* Right now, if you had a daughter, would you give her a different answer? Explain.

* How does dating a non-Christian affect how you feel about yourself? About God? About your relationship with God?

* Think of the friend that you respect the most. Would he or she agree with you?

* How about an adult that you really look up to – would they agree with you?

❋ Real Girls

❋ Real Guys

What happens when the "knight in shining armor" gets "tossed from his horse"? Sure, he seems pretty cool at first. Maybe even downright charming. But after you get to know him a bit more, he's not all he seems. And you wish you had known better in the first place. Sound familiar? We asked our real girls:

What do you wish you had known about guys before you started dating?

Kathy W.: "Girls need to realize how different girls and guys are. Guys just have less mature views of relationships. And girls need to be careful not to go out with the first guy who likes them—they should get to know him a little bit first."

Christy G.: "I wish I had known how physical guys like to be. Whether they're Christian guys or non-Christian guys, guys are still guys and have a hard time holding back. So I've learned how important physical boundaries are."

Brittany H.: "I wish I had REALLY understood that most guys aren't after the same things in relationships as girls. I also wish I had known that guys can't read minds, and they don't always feel the same way that girls do."

Emily B.: "I wish I had known that guys are very visual and physical appearance means a whole lot more to guys than to girls. Girls don't realize that what they wear makes a difference. My dad interviews the guys I go out with because he knows how he was when he was a teenager."

Elaine W.: "Guys have feelings too. They're not just tough, like they pretend to be. So sometimes you have to look behind their actions to know what they're feeling. And girls should get to know guys before they go out with them. Don't always go out just because they're 'cute.'"

Erica M.: "They are very, very sneaky. Don't believe everything they say. Build a door to your heart and hide the key. Don't find your security in them. Go slow and play it safe."

Macall R.: "I wish I would have known how much guys care and think about sex. I don't think sex is on the minds of girls very much and I have been shocked at what guys really want from girls."

Emily C.: "Girls should know that guys aren't worth the time or energy in high school. Be focused on your relationship with God and your other friends first."

Flirting. For some it comes easy, for some it's pretty tough. But what do the objects of our affection feel? Do they like flirting, or does it make them feel uncomfortable? Is it a turn-on or a turn-off? Our real guys gave us the scoop when we asked them:

What do you most wish girls knew about their flirting?

Drew W.: "I'm not very outgoing, so when a girl initiates some conversation and flirting, it's better than keeping our distance and just staring at each other. But flirting also doesn't need to be overdone. Girls should be natural instead of trying to impress a guy. Too much flirting can be bad."

Michael K.: "I don't mind unless that girl has a boyfriend already or I'm trying to be serious and she's still joking around. But don't make flirting the thing you use to get a guy to like you."

Jonathan M.: "If a girl knows I like her, she needs to not flirt with other guys around me. And if a girl flirts with every guy she comes across, she isn't worth the time or money."

E.J. Y.: "I think girls who flirt usually end up making themselves look like idiots. Especially if they flirt with more than one guy. That's a total turn-off. A little bit is OK, but most girls go too far."

Brandon W.: "Flirting can be fun, but a lot of guys don't know when a girl is kidding. So girls need to be careful. And they shouldn't do it all the time. Especially since flirting is NOT the way to get a really great guy."

Chris J.: "Some guys don't know when a girl is kidding. Plus sometimes girls who flirt get hurt because the guys who are attracted to flirting sometimes aren't the nicest. So girls need to beware of what they're getting into."

Kevin C.: "I'm often accused of flirting too much myself, but I'm really not. Sometimes it's just me joking around or showing off. So just because I'm being nice to a girl doesn't mean I want to date her. But when girls flirt with guys, they need to know that guys don't always pick up on everything. If they're making a move, they need to make it."

mirror mirror

by Kara Powell and Kendall Payne

VENUS & MARS
Closer than You Think

WHY I WISH I HAD SAID NO
Point of No Return

CAUGHT IN THE ACT
Go Sin No More

Plus: How far would you go?
Now it's your turn to answer

Venus and Mars

Just last night, someone told me, "The difference between girls and guys is that girls want everything from one guy while guys want one thing from lots of girls."

There's some truth there. Girls tend to look to one guy to solve all their problems, protect them from all dangers, make them feel special, and throw flowers their way on a regular basis. Guys seem to be more preoccupied with sex than girls.

It's been said that guys use love to get sex. And girls use sex to get love.

Maybe an overstatement, maybe a stereotype, maybe not so far from the truth. But girls want sex too. We're not coffee tables. We're human beings with real, pumping hormones.

I think about sex like a big pot of hot water. It's already pretty steamy, and maybe even close to boiling. If a girl doesn't like herself, it's like turning on the flame under that pot of hot water. She'll look to sex, or just going farther than she intended, as a way to feel better about herself. And for those minutes on that bed or couch, she will probably feel better about herself.

But soon the pot boils over. And then she gets burned.

Kari knew that the hard way. She's an eleventh grader who had been dating Steve for five months. Steve's mom asked Kari to help her throw Steve a surprise birthday party. Kari was happy to do it, both to honor Steve and to get to know his mom better.

The party went great, but it also ran late. Since it was 1:45 a.m. by the time they got everything cleaned up, Steve's mom asked Kari if she wanted to spend the night in their guest room so she wouldn't have to drive home so late. Kari called her mom and her mom said that was OK, as long as Steve's mom was there and Kari slept in the guest room.

Kari said goodnight to Steve and his mom and went to the guest room. She had been asleep for about an hour when Steve quietly knocked and came into the room. They started kissing hard, harder than they had kissed before. One thing lead to another and they slept together.

Kari had no intention of sleeping with Steve. In fact, she was planning on waiting until she got married. But it just felt so right, and being with Steve made her feel so loved and good about herself that it just happened.

Kari came to me two weeks later. She explained what happened, and then in tears, moaned, "And now Steve won't even return my calls. I thought he cared about me, but he only really cared about sex."

I cried with her. Not just because of her pain, but because I had seen it so many times. Girls using kissing, and French kissing, and fondling, and stroking, and eventually full blown sex to feel better about themselves. But in the end, they just feel dirty.

This chapter is full of people like Kari, people who went too far sexually. Whether or not it was their choice, the gift of sex that God intended to bring intimacy between husband and wife has instead become something that makes them feel far away from God, others, and even themselves.

But there's also good news in this chapter. There's grace, and forgiveness, and hope. Because there's Jesus.

So whether you're a virgin or you've slept with so many guys that you can't even remember their names, read on. There's a story waiting for you.

Never Been Kissed

By Kendall

Do you remember the movie from a few years back called "Never Been Kissed" (starring Drew Barrymore, Molly Shannon and David Arquette)? Well I do. It was the first movie my song had ever been in, which was really exciting. I was invited before the movie was even released to see a special screening of it. I took my best friend B. We went to a Hollywood back lot and crammed into a tiny movie theater with only 20 seats in it.

The president of Capitol records was there and a couple of other musical artists who also had songs in the movie. As the film began I found myself caught up in the funny characters and semi-interesting plot. Pretty soon I forgot why I was even there. And then I heard my song blasting through the speakers. A huge smile crept over my face and B and I turned to each other, clapping our hands, and giggling hysterically. Then the moment passed and we went back to watching.

Back to High School

My song wasn't the only reason I remembered that movie. The story was simple, a 25-year-old female reporter goes undercover posing as a high school student to find something newsworthy that might get her a promotion. She is forced to face the traumatic memories from her own high school years.

There were some powerful and embarrassing flashback scenes that really made you sympathize with her. I was amazed that Drew Barrymore even allowed herself to be shown on screen looking like she did! She was the ULTIMATE nerd. Bad hair, bad complexion, bad braces, bad figure, everything bad on the outside. But on the inside she was kind, intelligent, artistic, sensitive, and just downright beautiful. I couldn't help but feel connected to her.

Never Even Kissed? What's Wrong with You?

In the beginning of the movie she is conversing with her co-workers about their sexual experiences, when she blurts out unashamedly, "I've never been kissed". The awe, the horror, the confusion that filled their faces was obvious. "Who by the age of 25 has never been kissed? What's wrong with her?" You could see the wheels turning in their heads.

"What was wrong with her?" I asked myself. She had graduated from college, and pursued both a career and her passion, journalism. She'd landed a job doing what she actually loved. She had hobbies and other interests. Not the coolest—she enjoyed cross-stitching! She loved her family and had meaningful friendships. But for some reason all this paled in comparison to the wretched truth that she was 25 and had never even been kissed.

Boys...the Key to Your "Happily Ever After"?

We are constantly bombarded with the idea that in order to feel complete you must have a boyfriend, lover, husband, or at least a crush. And if you don't have that your life is void of meaning and excitement.

We are almost never presented with the idea by Hollywood that singleness is a gift and should be treated as one. It is always "the plague" upon someone. And the climax of the story is the moment when "true love" is realized. Then the screen fades to black and the script rolls in every woman's head "...and they lived happily ever after," accompanied by a sigh of delusional romanticism.

We think to ourselves, that's what I want. And the cycle is repeated. And the sickness is allowed to go on untreated. And we wind up either frustrated at our singleness or, frustrated at our boyfriends for not being the man we saw up there on that screen.

Spin the Bottle

Can you imagine waiting 25 years for your first kiss? Most girls have their first kiss by the age of 12. If not, definitely by 13. That was the way it was in my junior high. Games like "Spin the Bottle" and "Truth or dare" became the after school thing to do. Even on school trips when we were given free time, we'd all find a place to sit in a circle and the games would begin. Everyone was curious, and hey, curiosity's normal. Right?

Fortunately I was not the most popular or attractive of girls at my school. So no one ever dared anyone to kiss me. At the time I remember being devastated (now I'm grateful)!

Missed Opportunity or Simply Savoring the Flavor?

In the book *Reaching Out*, Henri Nouwen quotes a young student reflecting on his own experience; "When loneliness is haunting me with its possibility of being a threshold instead of a dead end, a new creation instead of a grave, a meeting place instead of an abyss, then time loses its desperate clutch on me. Then I no longer have to live in a frenzy of activity, overwhelmed and afraid for the missed opportunity."

What he's saying is that when you view your singleness as a gift, not a curse, your life will take on new meaning. When you stop worrying about when your first, second or hundredth kiss is coming you will actually enjoy it more when it comes. If you've never been kissed, or never had your first love, don't rush into it! Get to know yourself before you let anyone else know you.

The Snake Circle

By Kendall

The snake circle. In my mind I see a monster. I call it the snake circle.

Think of one snake in the shape of a capitol letter "C" And now think of another snake in the same "C" only flipped the other way so they over lap. One snake's head is eating the other snake's tail. Only the second snakes head is eating the first snakes tail. They are both feeding off each other and yet destroying each other at the same time.

The first snake is every man's battle with lust. And the second snake is every woman's battle with insecurity. They feed off each other.

I think of it as a two-headed monster. One head belongs to insecurity and the other to lust. But they feed the same beast. A woman will wear certain clothes and doll herself up, so that the outside looks confident and secure, but the inside is aching and longing to be loved. And a man will be drawn to the visual temptations of a sexy woman and never scratch under the surface.

Sex is good, or so I'm told. It seems, as a young person, the only place I hear that message is on MTV. For too long, Christians have placed sex in the "taboo" box and just say...you can open that when you're married—and that's about it.

Our Sex-Charged Culture

Meanwhile, the culture we are immersed in is pumping us chock full of images and thoughts of lifestyles that appear so enticing, risky, and normal that we can hardly resist. You can't walk down a street without being bombarded with at least 10 images involving sexual content.

TV shows present sexual encounters with friends, co-workers and even strangers as completely normal. You can turn on your TV any night of the week on any prime time station and learn about almost every sexual perversion there is.

You might wonder how I could talk about such things but really if we don't talk about them then who will?

I once heard a speaker say that the problem is that "the world tells the lie very well, while Christians tell the truth poorly." Now if the church and if we as Christians don't talk about these things, they will stay shameful and a thing of the "world"—the lie will be heard and embraced if truth never gets on the stage and grabs the microphone.

Sheer Curiosity Drives Most People Crazy

The other day I stopped by my boyfriend's house. On the kitchen table there was a brown paper bag, folded at the top. I casually asked what was in the bag. He just smiled and said, "can't tell you," in that little sing-songy, mocking voice.

"That's not fair," I said.

"Too bad," he retorted.

"I would rather you not say anything than tell me I can't know." At first I thought I'd get it out of him by demanding. When I saw that didn't work, I moved on to sweetness.

"Pleeasse tell me what's in the bag."

"Nope," he'd say, as cold as a stone.

"But I love you... and love is sharing... and we should share everything."

Then he smiles that little smirk that makes me believe he might give in.

"Its a surprise though," he said, "And I was going to wrap it. Are you sure you want it now?"

"Yeah, I'm sure."

Then he laughs, grabs the bag, and runs into his room, slamming the door behind him shouting, "You'll never know! you'll never know!"

I was so annoyed.

Its like if I say, "Don't think of a pink elephant." What's your first response, without even trying? To think of a pink elephant. It's human nature to have the 9 out of 10 things in your possession, yet forget about them all because you want the one you don't have.

Sex is out there for all. And sometimes it seems like everyone is out there enjoying it. And that can drive us nuts. It goes all the way back to the first man and woman. God gives them everything and yet they want the one thing they "can't" have ("dig the COOL tree!").

Insecurity...the Shiny Silver Beast

I must admit that the greatest struggle of my life is the daily battle with insecurity. I wake up in the morning and face, as my friend Jason calls it, the shiny silver beast. The mirror. It decides for me if I'm going to have a good day or bad.

Silly, isn't it? Why should I look in the mirror and tell myself I'm not thin enough or beautiful enough and then spend the whole day feeling self-conscious and less than I am. I think every single one of my female friends would agree that hands-down, the battle with insecurity rages daily. It seems to plague women as a gender. I have yet to meet a woman who lives in American society who doesn't desire to be beautiful and attractive to a man. And I also can gather from every man I've ever dared to have an intimate conversation with, that lust is the parallel struggle. What an interesting fight we are all engaged in.

Why I wish I had said No

By Marissa

Wow, six years ago. It's hard to believe that at 15, I had the ability to make a decision that would affect the rest of my life. I thought it would help our relationship. I thought it would make him love me more. I thought it was a way of solidifying our relationship so that no one else could take my place. (Or should I say, so that he wouldn't cheat on me again.)

Sharing the precious of gift of my virginity was not something that I planned to do. There's only one reason it happened. I was insecure. Instead of feeling like I was lovable all by myself, I thought that being physically intimate (in the deepest way possible) was what would make me worthwhile in his eyes.

At first, things seemed so good. Maybe this was the key to making my relationship better! Yeah, right. A couple of months after we first slept together, I found out that my boyfriend wasn't even a virgin like he said AND he was still cheating on me. How could he do this to me? How could I not see this? He said he loved me. Is this what love really is?

It took me quite a while to actually realize and muster up the courage to say no to him and the lies once and for all. Looking back on it, I think our sexual relationship was one of the reasons I could never let go of him. My worth was based on what he thought of me. And the only way I thought I could get him to still want me was sex.

Sex was something I used to make myself more lovable, bearable, and "good enough." The thing I didn't realize was that the exact opposite came true. Instead of becoming more confident and assured, I fell into a cycle of jealousy, anger, and envy. I was jealous of those who had the inner strength to be secure with themselves, angry because I was so mad at myself for letting my insecurity come to this, and envious of others who didn't "have" to use sex to make their boyfriend love them.

Today, I still struggle with my self-image. I have to constantly remind myself that I am worthy of love and respect just because I am me, because I am a child of the living God. I've tried sex and a whole bunch of other things, and they've all failed to plug that hole in my heart. Anything but God is a meager substitute and lie that will never fulfill the longing in my heart to know that I am loved and worth something.

Think about it:

* What's your first reaction to what you just read? (Really think about it for a minute or two.) Why did you react as you did?

* Can you relate to this girl's experience? Why?

* If you were Marissa's best friend in high school and you knew this was going on, what would you have done? Said?

* God created Marissa, and loves her very much, no matter what she's done. How do you imagine God reacted to Marissa's experience? What do you imagine he would say to her, had she turned to him in high school? What would he say to her now?

* Think of a friend you know who may be weighing a decision like the one Marissa made. What one thing will you do to try and help your friend avoid Marissa's sad mistake?

How Far Would You Go?

When it comes to dating, a big question is How far would you go? Now it's your turn to answer. There is a list below of how far some people may be willing to go, from least intimate to most intimate.

Do this:

1. Write a "G" before each act of physical intimacy that matches how far you think you'll go with a guy by the time you graduate from high school.

2. Write a "M" before each act of physical intimacy that matches how far you think you'll go with a guy before you get married.

(In case you didn't figure it out, G stands for Graduation and M stands for Marriage. Everybody say "Ah-hah.")

1. Hugging
2. Hand-holding
3. Massaging
4. Light kissing
5. Heavy kissing
6. Caressing
7. I'll show you mine if you'll show me yours
8. Mutual masturbation (masturbation is defined at right)
9. Oral sex
10. Sexual intercourse

Think about it...

* Why do you think you put the "G" and the "M" where you did?

* Is there a difference between the "G" and "M"? Why?

* If a friend came to you and asked you for advice about how far is OK to go before she gets married, what would you say? Why?

* Are your "G" and "M" any different than someone who has never read the Bible? How?

* Are your "G" and "M" any different than someone who wants to do exactly what the Bible says? How?

Since this is a book about self-image, and not just sex, we should probably talk about the way we feel about ourselves as well.

Now do this:

Go back to the list of sexual acts and...

1. **Circle the level of physical intimacy that matches how far you would go with a guy if you had perfect self-image and really liked yourself.**

2. **Underline the level of physical intimacy that matches how far you would go if you had lousy self-image and really hated yourself.**

Think about this too...

* Is there a difference between what you circled and what you underlined? Why?

* How did your feelings about yourself influence what you put "G" and "M" by at the top of the page?

Masturbation can be defined as touching your genitals to stimulate yourself.

The word "masturbation" is not found in the Bible, so Christians tend to have all sorts of different opinions about it. Some people think it is always wrong because it leads to visualizing someone of the opposite gender, which they define as lust. Other Christians say it's OK and normal as a way to release sexual pressure. A third group falls somewhere in the middle and says it might be OK at times, but it can easily become addictive and controlling, so try to stay away from it. .

Did You Know...

One out of every ten high school students was a victim of dating violence in the last 12 months.

(Child Trends Data Bank, 2002.)

Think about this...

* What do you think about masturbation?
* Is it always a bad thing to do, some-
* times a bad thing to do, or a good thing to do?
* If someone has a poor self-image, do you think they are more, or less, likely to try masturbation?
* If you've ever masturbated, how does it make you feel about yourself?
* What do you think is God's opinion about the matter?

I Said No!

By Anonymous

I said no. He didn't stop. I screamed, I yelled, I cried, but nothing would make him listen. I fought with all my might, but he was too strong for me. I kept telling myself over and over, "This isn't really happening. It's not happening to me, not to me," but it was.

It was the summer between my freshman and sophomore years in high school. I was raped. I was 14.

What had started out as an innocent flirtation earlier that day, ended in rape. In one day, I went from feeling pretty and worthy of affection to feeling ugly, betrayed and worthless. In one day, my life was shattered because I said no and he didn't listen.

I was on a family vacation in Alaska with my parents, my sister, and my brother. We'd been driving in the car for days and the longer we spent together, the less I liked anyone in my family. It was as if being in the car together magnified everything annoying about my parents, my sister's voice (which had risen a few octaves) and my brother's smell (worse than ever).

Mark opened a closet door and pulled me inside. At first I just figured we were going in there so we wouldn't get caught kissing, but then I realized what was happening.

All I wanted to do was get away from them, but seeing as how we were thousands of miles away from home, it didn't seem possible. Until the day I got freedom. . . well, at least a little.

In Alaska, they rely heavily on ferry boats for transportation between coastal cities. It's a little like a small cruise ship (well maybe not that nice), except you drive your car right onto it. We'd been on ferry boats already on our vacation, but only for a few hours here and there. This trip was going to be about 30 hours long.

I could smell freedom in the ocean air. My dad gave me permission to do what I wanted, as long as I reported back at a certain time. I was gone before he even finished his sentence. All I knew is that I wanted to put as much distance as possible between me and my family.

I wandered around each of the three decks for a while and discovered I liked the top deck the best. The wind in my face and the noise of the engine drowned out and drove away all the frustration I was having with my family. Although there were people around—sitting on deck chairs, taking pictures, looking at the scenery—I was all alone and I thought that it couldn't get much better. I was wrong.

A few minutes after I started enjoying my solitude, two guys came up and introduced themselves. I'd noticed they were on the deck when I first got up there; these guys were attractive and I tended to notice these things. They had been with a larger group of students, laughing, talking and having a good time.

I'd thought when I first saw the group that I'd like to be a part of the fun, but then reminded myself that I wasn't all that entertaining to be around, so I shrugged it off. But here were these guys, introducing themselves to me!

Their names were Mike and Mark and they explained that when they saw me, they really just wanted to meet me. I was blown away. No one had ever told me that before—and here they were, two good-looking guys, pursuing me.

Continued on next page...

Now I was sure—life couldn't get much better than this. The guys brought me back to the group and introduced me, and we all hung out and laughed for about an hour. Then Mike and Mark decided to treat me to some great Ferry Boat food (it's very similar to school cafeteria food — the word 'great' is said very sarcastically).

Before long, our meal conversation turned a little risqué. I tried to steer the conversation back, but every time I did, one of them brought it right back to where it was before. The guys were joking about sexual stuff and I didn't want to seem like a prude, so I just joined right in. It made me a little uncomfortable, but I ignored those feelings.

After the guys had a brief whispered conversation, Mark asked me if I wanted to go for a walk. I'd found him to be the more attractive of the two, so I was delighted.

As we walked around the deck, he said a lot of nice things to me. He told me I was pretty. He told me he was lucky to have met me. I'd never heard such great things out of a cute guy's mouth! I was really excited. Along our walk he stopped, looked into my eyes, and kissed me. My heart was beating so fast. I was in love.

Mark suggested we go to a more secluded part of the ship. I readily agreed. I was enjoying being around him so much that I didn't really think about much else.

We got to a dark hallway and began kissing again. It wasn't like before. It wasn't nice and soft; the kissing and the touching was actually a little uncomfortable. I wasn't very experienced at kissing and stuff, so I just thought it was my not knowing what to do that made it awkward. I tried to relax and enjoy it -- after all, people I knew always talked about making out for hours, so I figured it had to get better.

It didn't. Mark opened a closet door and pulled me inside. At first I just figured we were going in there so we wouldn't get caught kissing, but then I realized what was happening. Mark threw me on the ground and was on top of me before I knew it.

I was stunned for a moment and then I started fighting back. I said No. I told him to stop. He ignored me and started ripping my clothes. I yelled at him to stop and then I just started to scream, and then he hit me.

Continued on next page...

He hit me right across the face. He told me to shut up. He told me that I led him on and I was asking for this.

I was confused. I was stunned. And hurt. I started to cry. I fought back and tried to get away, but he was too strong for me. After a few minutes, which seemed like hours, he was done with me. He got up and walked out without saying a word.

I heard the closet door close and I didn't know what to do. I wanted to throw up. I wanted to go after him and cause him pain. I wanted to run to someone who would protect me. But all I did was curl up and cry. I don't know how long I was there.

Eventually I started back to where my parents were staying. I ran into my father on the way and he just started yelling at me. I'd missed the deadline he'd given me to check in and he thought I'd run away. He told me that he didn't want to hear my excuse, and he was tired of me being so selfish, and trying to tear the family apart. I made the decision right there in the hallway of the ferry boat that I was never going to tell anyone what happened to me. I would just pretend like it didn't happen.

I got through the rest of that vacation and somehow managed to keep my secret for the next four years. I dated a little in high school, but never let anyone get too close to me — personally or physically.

When I was in college, I started seeing this guy I really liked. He seemed gentle and Christlike enough to accept me and like me, even with all my baggage. I started to let my guard down.

One night we were in a loud restaurant with a bunch of our friends and he was trying to get my attention. He reached over and grabbed me from behind in a playful gesture, but before I knew what was happening, I turned around and slugged him and knocked him on the ground.

I wasn't in control. My body reacted before my brain could throw any logic into the situation. I tried to explain away my actions as if it were all a big joke—but I knew better, on the inside. As suddenly as he grabbed me, all the memories I had been pushing down for years came rushing up. I was suddenly a scared, hurt, used, and dirty 14-year-old all over again.

That night when I got home, I cried like never before. Why did something that happened so long ago have to be haunting me now?

I soon sought out professional help from a Christian therapist. She and I worked through many of my feelings and memories that surrounded this trauma. A couple of months into my therapy, she suggested I attempt to forgive Mark. I fought the idea at first, but a few weeks later I chose to forgive and I actually prayed for Mark's healing in this situation.

I thought that the forgiveness of my attacker would be the toughest part of my healing. It was tough. There are times I want to take it all back, but once again, I was wrong. I had to forgive myself.

For years, I had thought it was my fault. I believed I truly had led him to a place where he couldn't stop and that I was guilty of having sex before marriage. To this day, I have a hard time of thinking myself pure. I have worked in the church with students for a while and whenever the subject of virginity comes up, I cringe. I know that God sees me as a virgin, but I don't know how to explain it to others.

If I had to explain how I feel about myself because of my rape, I would say "worthless." I don't feel good enough when I am around strong Christians who seem to have it all together. I don't feel deserving of compliments.

Relationships with guys? I'm real good at being their friend — but if it even hints at being more than that, I sub-consciously sabotage the relationship. I don't want to experience their disappointment when they discover all that comes with me if they get to know me too well.

What happened to me was merely one night of my life, but I've been dealing with it ever since. There are days when I feel dirty, guilty, and worthless… and there are days that I understand a fragment of God's love for me. God sees me as a worthy child. He loves me and embraces me with the fact that he allowed His son to die on the cross for me. I look forward to spending more days seeking the knowledge that I am loved, saved, and made pure by Jesus Christ.

The Diary of a Youth Pastor

1 a.m. phone calls are never good. Ever.

And last night's was no exception. It was Ben. I've spent a lot of time with Ben lately, especially since he joined our small group. He's been coming to our church for about a year now, asking a lot of great questions about God. In June, he decided to ask Jesus to take over his life. It's not like Ben's life is perfect now, but he likes reading the Bible and praying.

I was pretty excited when Ben started dating Kristin. Kristin is super solid. She's been going to our church forever. She hasn't dated much, but I could tell she liked Ben. She tried to be sly about it, but I knew what was up even before they told me that they were officially dating.

I could tell as soon as Ben said last night, "It's me, Ben," that something was wrong. He didn't sound like himself. He sounded shaky. Scared. Nervous.

"I did something really bad tonight."

"What?" I asked.

"I don't know if I should tell you."

"It's cool, Ben. It can't be that bad."

"OK. I…ummm…slept with Kristin tonight."

I must have misunderstood him.

"What did you say?"

"I slept with Kristin."

"Wow," I said, in shock.

"Yeah."

"Look, Ben, let's get together and talk about it. Are you free for breakfast before school? Let's meet at the donut shop by the church at 6:30 a.m."

We both hung up. I don't know about Ben, but there was no way I was going back to sleep. I paced, and prayed, and sat, and paced, prayed, and sat all over again. I got out my Bible, and turned to a few verses I thought would help. Things I wanted to share with Ben.

Finally around 3 a.m., I went back to sleep. When my alarm went off at 6, I hopped in the shower, threw on some clothes, and headed off to meet Ben. He was already there. I wasn't sure if he'd be smiling or crying.

He did neither so I started talking.

"Ben, I've been praying for you so much since you called. I'm here for you. I'll support you. No matter what. What you did was wrong, but God and I both love you."

"That's good to hear," he said.

Then he paused, "There's something I've got to tell you. I never slept with Kristin. I just wanted to see how you would respond to me if I did."

Think about it...

* How would you feel if you were the youth pastor?

* Why do you think Ben told him that he had slept with Kristin?

* Let's say he did it because he was wondering if the youth pastor would still care about him even if he had blown it. Do you ever wonder the same thing about the adults in your life? When? Why?

* Who's an adult that would be there for you no matter what? If you can't think of anyone, how does that make you feel? Is there a friend's parent who you could talk to? A teacher? Coach? Someone at your church?

There's often a pretty vicious cycle that happens. You blow it sexually, you hide what happened from others, you feel bad about yourself, and so you blow it sexually again. For you who like pictures, try this:

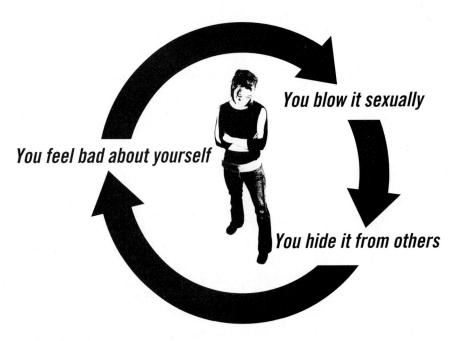

You blow it sexually

You feel bad about yourself

You hide it from others

Think about it...

* Have you ever done something sexually that you regret?

* What was your first instinct: to tell someone, or to hide it from others? Why?

* What did you end up doing? How did you feel?

* Let's say that you hid it from others. Do you think telling someone about it would change how you feel about yourself right now? Change the way they look at you?

* Let's say that you told someone. Do you think hiding it from others would change how you feel about yourself right now?

* Is there anything you need to talk about with an adult you respect in the next few weeks? What would keep you from doing that? What would you gain by doing that? What will you do today to make sure you have a talk with them?

Caught in the Act

Those eyes. They're not what I expected. I expected anger, or wrath. Instead I saw tenderness, compassion.

I got caught in the act. What had started as some innocent flirting with my neighbor had gone much further. Too far. When his wife was visiting her sister, he invited me over for dinner. I thought to myself, "What's the harm?"

Plenty. The wine, the candlelight, the warmth, it all got to me. And to him too. We ended up sleeping together. And then I fell asleep in his arms.

We woke up to some pounding on his front door. When he went to open it, some Jewish leaders rushed right past him, up the stairs, to the bedroom. I don't know how they knew what had happened, but they grabbed me, jerked me out of bed, told me to wrap the sheet around me, and forced me down the stairs and out the front door.

They rushed me toward the temple court. I had no choice but to go with them. Two men on either side of me were grabbing my arms, and I knew what was ahead. According to Leviticus 20, I should be stoned. They were taking me to a nice public place to make an example out of me.

I cried, I begged, I dragged my feet, but they wouldn't stop. On we went, toward the temple.

There was a man there, standing and teaching others, and we seemed to be headed toward him. I had never met him, but by the large crowds, I figured that this must be that famous Teacher named Jesus.

They threw me down at his feet. One of the more angry ones spoke up, "Teacher, this woman was caught sleeping with someone. You know that Moses commanded us to stone her and kill her. What do you say?"

My life was in his hands. I had heard that this Jesus was a compassionate person, but I also knew that he took the Scriptures seriously.

The silence was deafening. Jesus reached down, and with his pointer finger on his right hand, began to write something in the ground. From where I was kneeling, I couldn't see what it was.

More of my accusers chimed in. "Jesus, what's your verdict?" "Come on, quit stalling." "Stop writing and speak up."

Slowly he stood. Looking around at everyone else but me, he said, "If any of you has never made a similar mistake, go ahead and throw a stone at her."

More silence. Jesus went back to writing on the ground. My accusers looked at him, at the ground, at me, back at the ground. Some of the older guys walked away first. Then the younger ones.

It was just me and this Jesus. Me and my rescuer. Now I figured I'd get yelled at.

But there were those eyes. Firm in truth, but soft in love. "Go and sin no more" he said to me. I paused, letting what he said register in my brain. Go? I'm free?

Sin no more? I know myself too well to think that's really going to happen. But I remember those eyes, and I know what they would want me to do. They'd want me to stop sleeping with other people, and keep myself for marriage.

I might not have sex with anyone else before I get married, but I'm sure I'll do some other bad stuff. And what then? Those eyes carry the answer. "Go and sin no more," they'll say again and again and again.

"Go and sin no more." Five very powerful words that Jesus said to a woman caught in adultery in John 8:1-11.

Think about it:

* Think of something you've done sexually, that you regret. Picture those same eyes looking at you. Hear Him saying, "Go and sin no more." How do you feel?

* How are you to respond? What should you say or do?

* Do you think you'd make the same mistake again? Why?

* When you make a mistake, sexual or not, what do you think Jesus would want you to do?

* Let's say the woman kept sleeping around, and Jesus heard about it. Do you think he'd ever get so angry with her that He'd want nothing more to do with her? Why?

* Lots of girls find that if they go farther than they'd like with a guy, they're more likely to do it again in the future. Has that been true for you?

* How does repeating the same sexual mistake make you feel about yourself?

* How would you feel about yourself if you lived up to Jesus' command to go and sin no more?

* If you commit sexual sin, what is the first thing you should do? What things should you do to be sure to "go and sin more"? Who should you speak with to help you stand strong?

* How has this account of Jesus and the woman encouraged you? What will you differently from now on as a result?

*Real Girls

*Real Guys

You just read that for the average guy, love is mostly just a way to get sex. But what about girls? Is the flipside true for us? Do we use sex and physical intimacy as a way to feel close to guys? Let's get the lowdown from our real girls:

Is it true that girls, in general, use sex to get love or feel loved?

Kathy W.: "I think girls definitely cross physical boundaries so they can feel loved and special. Girls will do things that we normally wouldn't do in order to feel accepted."

Christy G.: "At my school, girls are pretty physical with guys. They will do just about anything with a guy to feel loved. But in the end, they get hurt because after the guys 'get some,' they move on."

Brittany H.: "I think that is totally true. And it's not just sex. Girls use kissing and other physical stuff as reassurance that someone likes them."

Emily B.: "At my school and in my group of friends, I don't think it's true, but I'm not really sure. I know some girls would do it though."

Elaine W.: "Yeah, it's true. A lot of girls want to have that 'special feeling' of being in love so they'll try anything."

Erica M.: "They won't always have sex, but girls will do physical stuff to get closer to boys."

Searcy C.: "Yea, sadly enough. If not sex, then other stuff, if you know what I mean. A lot of girls want to please the guy and then they do it."

Macall R.: "I think it's very true and most of the time girls don't even realize what they're doing. Girls want love so much that they will do anything to feel that someone cares about them."

Nicole R.: "Girls do use guys and sex to make them feel better about themselves."

Emily C.: "Yes, because most girls think being loved is a bigger deal than physical stuff, so they'll use physical intimacy as a way to feel important and loved."

The flowers. The dinner. The movie. The romantic conversation. Does the guy really like you, or does he have something else on his mind? We wanted to know, so we asked our real guys whether it's true that guys, in general, use love to get sex. In other words, are guys nice to us just so that they can score with us? Our real guys were gut-level honest. And while they're nicer than the average guy, they gave us the low-down on where guys, in general, are coming from.

Is it true that guys use love to get sex?

E.J. Y.: "Most high school guys do use love to get sex. But there are a few who don't. You can usually tell what a guy thinks about sex. If he's had lots of girlfriends, then he's probably after sex."

Jonathan M.: "For most of the guys at my school, all they think about is how far they can get with a girl."

Drew W.: "Every day at my school I see guys use love to get sex. It happens a lot, and I don't think girls realize it."

Michael K.: "I think that guys ultimately want sex, one way or the other. Guys talk about getting to 'first base,' 'second base,' 'third base,' and then ultimately 'home.' I guess guys are just like that."

Brandon W.: "It's sad to say, but I guess the average high school guy does use love to get sex. If a girl really wants love, she needs to know that guys might be using romance as a way to sleep with her."

Kevin C.: "Guys are highly driven by sex, anywhere and at any time. At our church, the guys will probably be a little more respectful, but if you're looking for guys at parties, you're going to get more than you want."

Chris J.: "It happens a lot at parties. Especially if people are drinking. Girls and guys will sleep together, but it's not a relationship that guys really want. It's just about sex."

mirror mirror

by Kara Powell and Kendall Payne

friends
— AND —
accountability

✱ **11 DAYS**
Anything You Need to Talk About?

✱ **CONTROL**
A Journal Records the Struggle

✱ **IF ONLY SOMEBODY HAD ASKED ME**
A Story of Biblical Proportions

Plus: Questions that good friends ask each other

Account-a-what???

ac·count a·bil i·ty—(1) Giving an account; (2) Inviting others to speak into your life; (3) Doing a risky thing to make sure you stay on the right track.

When my brother was little, he wanted to be a stop sign. Not a very lofty career goal, but hey, when you're four, stop signs seem pretty powerful.

Odds are good that you could use a few more stop signs in your life. Or maybe some more "slow down" or "caution" signs. You might be cruising a little too fast, or maybe heading down the wrong road, and if someone doesn't stop you, you're going to crash and burn.

That's where accountability comes in. It's all those definitions listed at the top of this page and lots more. Basically, accountability happens when you admit that you need help. You have questions. You have some answers, but you're not sure they're the right ones.

And sometimes it even happens when you don't want it to happen. It happens when some brave friend taps you on the shoulder (or maybe gives you a body blow) and gives you their opinion on what you're thinking or doing.

Why is it important in a book about self-image? First off, by now you might want to change some things about yourself, and you'll need people to support you as you do it. Second, some of your ideas about yourself are probably pretty whacked, and you need someone to shout out a reality check. If you're like most of us, you've probably got lots of lies about who you are and how you look running rampant in your head or out your mouth. If someone doesn't speak up with the truth, it could get ugly.

So are you still a bit fuzzy on what accountability mean? Here are a few ideas that might clear it up a bit:

Here are a few ideas that might clear it up a bit.

1. When you think a friend is making a mistake, tell her, not others.
If there's one thing teenage girls are good at, it's gossip. When we think Suzy is making a mistake by dating Brad, we tell Kimberly and Kiki and Steve. But we don't tell Suzy. Let's change that. If we have concerns about something Suzy has done, or is doing, or is thinking about doing, let's tell Suzy first.

2. Instead of figuring it'll happen sometime, set a specific time.
Like lots of relationships, if we just assume that accountability will squeeze in somewhere, it's likely to get squeezed out. Once you've figured out which friends you want to invite to speak into your life, and what friends need you to speak into theirs, decide when to talk to them about it. Maybe after school on the bus. Or maybe when you spend the night on Friday night. You might like it so much that you decide to talk every week or two.

3. If you're too busy for something superficial, it's your job to go deep.
Think of accountability like a swimming pool. You can choose to dive in at the deep end and share what's really going on, or you can splash around in the shallow end and stay pretty surfacey. Instead of just talking about who you're hoping asks you to the winter formal, you share how afraid you are that no one will ask you. Instead of just sharing how angry you are with your dad, you let your friends know how much it hurts you when he misses your soccer games. Maybe you're the one who is going to set the tone for your friends.

We all need people in our lives whose opinions, advice, and friendship have been proven over time. People with whom we can be absolutely real and transparent. People who can be trusted to gently prod us and sometimes guide us in our Christian walk. Read on to discover more about friendship and accountability.

Got Fleas?

By Kendall

I was driving someone to the airport early one morning, being a good friend. When the airport is 45 minutes away you only call your "good friends" to pick you up and drop you off. So you know when you are asked the question you are pretty much obligated.

Half awake, I had just exited the 405 freeway merging onto a surface street when a sign caught my eye. It said in black bold letters, "Got Fleas?" Maybe it was the early morning delirium, but it struck me as hysterically funny. I itched my head in a reactionary response. Soon I realized it was in front of a pet store (which made sense) and it was yet another attempt to piggyback the "got milk?" ad campaign. How many more will there be? Got Milk? Got God? Got Fleas? Got a new slogan yet?

Anyways it reminded me of a story my mom told me long ago. The story of a woman named Corrie ten Boom. Her Dutch family hid Jews in a secret hiding place at the top of her family's house during Hitler's reign. When they were discovered, she and her sister, Betsie, were sent to a Nazi concentration camp even though they were Christians. She retells their story in a book called *The Hiding Place*, recounting Gods great faithfulness and love even in the most desperate situations.

The excerpt below finds the two women having just arrived at the final concentration camp called Ravensbruck. The conditions were horrible. The smell of backed up toilets filled the air. Ten to 12 women were forced to share a bed. The bedding reeked, and was soiled and rancid. The place smelled so bad that nausea would sweep over them regularly. Filth covered everything. On top of this, fleas swarmed throughout the entire place, feasting on them almost non-stop.

"Fleas…Betsie, how can we live in such a place?"

"Show us. Show us how."

It was said so matter of factly it took me a second to realize she was praying…."Corrie!" She said excitely. "He's given us the answer! Before we asked, as He always does! In the Bible this morning. Where was it? Read that part again!"

I glanced down the long dim aisle to make sure no guard

was in sight, then drew the bible from its pouch. "It was in First Thessalonians," I said. In the feeble light I turned the pages. "Here it is: 'comfort the frightened, help the weak, be patient with everyone. See that none of you repays evil for evil, but always seek to do good to one another and to all…'"

"Go on," said Betsie. "That wasn't all."

"Oh yes: '…to one another and to all. Rejoice always, pray constantly, give thanks in all circumstances; for this is the will of God in Christ Jesus.'"

"That's it, Corrie! That's His answer. 'Give thanks in all circumstances!' That's what we can do. We can start right now to thank God for every single thing about this new barracks!"

I stared at her, and then around me at the dark, foul-aired room.

"Such as?" I said.

"Such as being assigned here together."

I bit my lip. "Oh yes, Lord Jesus!"

"Such as what you're holding in your hands."

I looked down at the bible. "Yes! Thank you, dear Lord, that there was no inspection when we entered here! Thank you for all the women, here in this room, who will meet you in these pages."

Continued on next page…

"Yes," said Betsie. "Thank you for the very crowding here. Since we're packed so close, that many more will hear!" She looked at me expectantly. "Corrie!" she prodded.

"Oh, all right. Thank you for the jammed, crammed, stuffed, packed, suffocating crowds."

"Thank you," Betsie went on serenely, "for the fleas and for…"

The fleas! This was way too much. "Betsie, there's no way even God can make me grateful for a flea."

"'Give thanks in all circumstances.'" She quoted. "It doesn't say, 'in pleasant circumstances.' Fleas are part of this place where God has put us." And so we stood between piers of bunks and gave thanks for fleas. But this time I was sure Betsie was wrong.

The sisters, with timidity, started a worship "service" in their dorm. Before long, they had so many people attending that they added a second service after evening roll call. Normally such meetings would have been prevented and punished due to normally rigid surveillance of guards and others.

Over time they discovered that the Germans would not enter their dorm for any reason…because of the fleas. Corrie writes, "My mind rushed back to our first hour in this place. I remembered Betsie's bowed head, remembered her thanks to God for creatures I could see no use for."

The first time I heard that story I cried, each subsequent time I have cried, and even now it brings tears to my eyes. I remember I was 14 years old. There were two cute boys in my youth group and I wanted to marry either one of them, it did not matter which. They were both 17 and had their drivers' licenses. The only reason they barely even knew that I existed was because I was a family friend of a girl in the group who happened to be beautiful. They thought she was hot and I was her friendly sidekick. When they would talk to her I would hang around and try to be a part of their circle.

One Sunday morning I went to church hoping they would invite me to a lunch outing I had overheard them planning. I had dreamt all week that they would include me. I had told all my school friends about how cute these guys

were. I had my outfit planned since Monday night. I got up extra early to make sure my hair and makeup looked the best I knew how to do it.

I will never forget the feeling of seeing them drive off together without me. I fought the tears back all the way home, ran up to my room and slammed my door. I flung myself on the floor and cried huge, salty tears. True, it was not a concentration camp but it sure felt like one at that point. It felt like my life was over. There came a quiet knock on my door, followed by the face of my mother peering through the crack as she opened it.

"Do you want to talk?" She said.

"No" I said, trying to sniff and soak up the tears on my sleeve. She sat down next to me and started to talk anyway. It was here that she told me about Corrie and Betsie and the fleas.

At the end of the story she looked at me and said, "You have to thank God for theses fleas! Thank Him for these times of sadness because it is these times that are going to write the songs that will speak to people so deeply. And it is when you feel forgotten, that you will write about the struggle. And when someone else feels that way they'll listen to your music or read your words and feel encouraged."

While the pain never leaves, and the sincere ache of loneliness I experienced has left a lasting scar, I can now see how God works all things for good.

What are your fleas? Is it your parents getting divorced? Is it the pimples on your face? Are you and a friend not talking? Do you have no boyfriend when all your other friends do? Did a friend betray you? It is at those moments and in those circumstances where you must thank God, knowing He always has a purpose and meaning behind everything even when we can't see it!

So you can imagine how ironic it was to see a sign on my way to the airport saying, "Got Fleas?" I thought yeah, still do! Thanks God!

If Only Somebody Had Asked Me...

By Sam

People say love makes you blind. I think it makes you blind and a little bit stupid.

I loved Dee. She was so beautiful and fun. And best of all, she loved me too. But maybe that's where the blindness comes in.

See, I was under a Nazirite vow, which meant that if I stayed away from wine, dead bodies, unclean food, and never cut my hair, I'd be super strong. It made me so strong that one time I killed a thousand guys from Philistia called Philistines. I was so strong that I led the people of Israel for twenty years. Even when the Philistines tried to capture me, I snuck out, and demolished part of their city.

Back to our love story...

The Philistines were pretty ticked at me, so it turns out that they went to Dee and asked her what made me so strong. Since she didn't know, they said they'd give her a bunch of cash if she found out and told them.

Three times she tried to get me to tell her what made me so strong. Each time I lied to her. I don't know why— maybe it was my own intuition, or maybe it was God. But I just knew that I shouldn't tell her what made me so strong.

But boy was she a whiner. She argued, "Sam, how can you say, 'I love you' when you won't tell me your secrets?" Day after day, she nagged me.

Finally, I told her everything. If anyone shaves my head, my strength would hit the road and I'd be like a normal guy.

That night she made me a really romantic dinner. And afterwards, I was so full that I fell asleep. I guess she let some Philistine guys into my house, and one of them shaved my head. They pounced on me, and when I tried to fight back, they beat me up. Normally I could have taken all eight of them with one hand tied behind my back, but this time I was too weak.

So here I sit in prison. All because I told my true love about my true strength.

I wish I had told my friends what Dee was up to. They probably would have been smarter than me and warned me.

And I wish Joey would have hung out more with me and asked me more questions about our relationship. He only lives a few doors down, but he's just so busy.

If only someone had asked me what was going on with Dee. If only someone had asked me how I was doing.

If you haven't guessed it by now, Sam is actually Samson, and Dee is actually Delilah. You can read their full story in the Bible in Judges 13-16. One warning: it's not a very happy ending. It'd probably get at least a PG-13 rating. Samson's hair grows back a bit, and when the Philistines take him into their temple, he pushes hard on the temple pillars, and the whole building comes tumbling down. He kills over 1,000 people, including himself. Makes you wonder, "If only someone had asked him...".

Eleven Days

By Anonymous

Thursday, September 20

Every time I'm with him, I do it. Or rather, we do it. We're not technically having sex, but it still doesn't feel right. It feels good, really good, but not right. I wish I could stop. I'll just have to try harder. Next time, I won't let him touch me like that.

Saturday, September 22

I love the flowers he gave me last night—white roses, my favorite. He looked so totally hot in that black leather jacket. And the date he planned was so romantic. A picnic in the park, and then dessert under the stars. I think I'm falling for him. He's so nice, and cute, and easy to talk to. Even Blanca likes him, and she's critical of just about everybody.

When he drove me back home, he parked a few houses away, just out of sight of my parents' curious looks. All day, I told myself, "Don't let him touch you there," like a zillion times in my brain. But after the great date he planned, I wanted him to.

Tuesday, October 16

After going out for six weeks, why am I still so insecure around him? He's so cool, and I'm just sort of OK. I guess deep down I can't believe that a guy like him would like me.

I think that's part of why I let him stroke me. It's like my hold over him. If we go farther physically, then he won't leave me. He'll like me. He might even need me.

Friday, October 19

I need help. We're doing more than just touching. Tonight he even unzipped his pants. How do I stop this?

Wednesday, October 24

I think my mom knows something is up. She keeps giving me that motherly look and saying, "Honey, is there something we need to talk about?" No way could I ever talk to my mom about it. It's too personal. Too private.

Thursday, October 25

I know: I'll make a promise to myself. If I let him touch me, then I have to give an extra $20 to my church. I can stop myself, and I sure don't want to lose twenty bucks.

Wednesday, October 31

He did it again. Actually, twice. And I haven't even given any extra money to my church.

Thursday, November 8

Michelle can tell something is wrong. She keeps emailing me, asking me if I'm OK. She says that during history class, I looked like I was worried about something. I told her it's no big deal, and then changed the subject.

Sunday, November 11

Maybe I should talk with Michelle. I think she'd understand. But what if she doesn't? What if she judges me? Or thinks I'm dirty or something?

Tuesday, November 13

I finally talked to Michelle today. We were on the bus home from school, and she asked me again, "Are you sure you're OK?" I told her what was wrong, and how dirty I felt, and how I wanted to stop. She just listened. She didn't try to give me any dumb advice. She just listened. As we turned the corner by her stop, she said she'd pray for me. And she wondered if it would be OK if she asked me how I was doing in a few days. She said that sometimes knowing someone is going to ask you about something makes you try a little harder.

Wednesday, November 21

I'm so glad I told Michelle. She's asked me twice this week how I'm doing. And just knowing she's going to ask me makes it so much easier to stop a little sooner when I'm in the back seat with him.

Think about it...

✳ When have you felt like you were doing something wrong, something you can't seem to stop doing? What made it so hard to stop?

✳ How did you stop doing it, or are you still doing it? How does that make you feel?

✳ Some people might call it an addiction to "do something wrong that you can't stop." Do you agree? Why?

✳ How did Michelle help in the story above? What else could she have done for her friend?

✳ Who are some people in your life who could do for you what Michelle did for her friend in the story?

✳ What one thing can you do to be more accountable to at least one of these people you listed?

✳ Is there anything you need to talk about with someone this week? Within the next hour or two, set up a time to talk with them. Don't put it off!

Control

By Cindi

I guess it was the earthquake that did it. It was inside me all the time, pent up, steaming, bubbling. But it erupted after the earthquake.

The earthquake terrified me. I like to be in control of things, and during an earthquake, nothing is in control. Streets ebb and flow like tidal waves. Buildings sway like trees. No place is solid.

And the shaking doesn't stop. Sure, it stops for a few hours here and there, but then the aftershocks come. They're almost as strong as the first quake.

With the ground around me trembling, I yearned for stability and control. In my life I was looking for something, anything, that I could control. That I could make mine. That I could protect and manage.

Food.

The perfect thing to try to control. I had all sorts of chances every day. At breakfast, would I control myself and just have half a bagel, or would I give in and also have a side of bacon? At dinner, could I restrain my hunger to just a salad, or did the mashed potatoes and roast beef make me weak?

It's not like I knew what I was doing. And it's not like I knew what I was getting into. It started small. My friends were having brownie sundaes for dessert. I felt kind of full already, so I passed. And as I sat surrounded by my chocolate-eating friends, I felt better about myself. I felt strong. I hadn't given in.

Then I moved from skipping dessert to skimping on the main meal. If I ate enough rice, I'd eat half as much chicken. If I piled on the lettuce, I was full by the time I turned to the macaroni and cheese.

It wasn't just about looking thin. People told me I already was thin. Some days I believed them, some days I didn't. But even on the days when I believed them, I still watched what I ate. I wanted to be thin because then I would have it all together.

Food and exercise go hand and hand, and for me, they linked arms every night around 5:00. It started out with Monday and Wednesday aerobics. Then I added Tuesday, Thursday and Friday soccer. It felt great to work out, to feel myself get stronger and thinner.

I'd even try to work out just before dinner. Then I could show up for the meal and feel like I had really earned it.

I never became technically anorexic. I studied Anorexia and Bulimia in my Psychology class, and I was only about half way there. I didn't have anorexia, but I had anorexic tendencies.

I remember having dinner with a bunch of friends from my church. Somehow we got talking about our favorite foods. One guy said, "I love food so much. I don't see how anyone could ever become anorexic. Bulimic, maybe, because then you get to eat what you want first."

My heart pounded harder. I needed to be by myself. Trying not to be too obvious, I excused myself and went to the bathroom. There in the stall, I sat and I cried.

No one ever knew. Until one day I told my friend Ginny.

How Do You Rate?

If you want good friends who help you with everything from how you feel about yourself to how you're going to stop smoking, you need to be a good friend. How do you rate on these qualities of friendship?

Do this: Read each of the friendship fruit in the chart below and rate yourself on that fruit, checking the 1, 2, or 3 box in the column that matches your response:

Friendship Fruit	1 Point Definitely not me	2 Points Kinda me	3 Points Totally me
Love: In general, I'm committed to doing the best for my friends, even if it means it costs me something.			
Joy: When a friend has something good happen, instead of being jealous, I'm genuinely happy for them.			
Peace: When a friend gets stressed, I listen to them and remind them everything's going to work out.			
Patience: When a friend hurts my feelings, I'm quick to forgive them and be friends again.			
Kindness: I encourage my friends, both about who they are and how they look.			
Goodness: I don't talk about my friends behind their backs.			
Faithfulness: I'm just as likely to stop and talk to my popular friends as I am my not-so-popular friends.			
Gentleness: If a friend does something pretty dorky, I laugh with her about it but try not to make fun of her.			
Self-control: When a friend tells me a secret, I throw it in the vault and don't tell others.			

Now add up your score.

9-15: Friendship Challenged

Face the facts: you've got some work to do. You may have some friends, but you could make yourself quite a bit friendlier. Choose two things to do differently this week to be a better friend. Ask a friend to hold you accountable for how you want to change.

16-21: Fair Weather Friend

As a friend, you've got your good days and your bad days. You may even think you're doing OK, but the truth is that there are lots of things you could be doing to become an even stronger, more faithful friend. Choose two things to do differently this week to be a better friend. Let someone else know how you're planning to improve. Ask them to hold you accountable by asking you at the end of the week how you did.

22-27: Friend Phenom

Hey, will you be our friend? Seriously, you know how to stick it out with your buds and be there for them when they need you. But there are always areas where you could improve. Think of one thing you'd like to do this week to be a better friend. Let someone know what that thing is so that they can hold you accountable for your goal.

To find out more about being a good friend, try a dose of Galatians 5:22-23, Acts 2:42-47, and Philippians 2:1-5.

Questions that good friends ask each other:

OK, we're not saying you have to go through all of these every time you hang out. But maybe you could pick a few of them to ask a good friend the next time you see them.

* What's going well in your life right now?

* What are you struggling with right now?

* Is that struggle harder now than it was a few weeks ago?

* How are you feeling about yourself? Why?

* What's one way your parents would want you to treat them differently?

* How are you treating your brothers and sisters?

* Are you being the kind of friend to others that you want them to be to you?

* What's going on in your relationship with God?

* What's one thing you could do this week to get to know God better?

* How have you served someone recently? Are you happy with your answer?

* Would other kids at school be able to tell by your actions alone that you're a follower of Christ? Why?

* What's going on physically with your boyfriend or girlfriend? How about emotionally?

* If you had to give yourself an overall purity grade, what would it be? Why?

* Anything else we need to talk about?

* Have you lied about anything you've told me?

Did You Know...

According to Marion Underwood, a professor of psychology at the University of Texas at Dallas, "Girls very much value intimacy, which makes them excellent friends and terrible enemies. They share so much information when they are friends that they never run out of ammunition if they turn on one another."
(Margaret Talbot, "Mean Girls," *The New York Times Magazine*, February 24, 2002, 26).

That means you better choose who you share with pretty carefully.

Real Guys

Are guys different when they're with Billy and Sammy than when they're with Betty and Suzie? Are they one way with their guy friends, but then act differently with us? We wanted to know, so we went right to the source. We asked our real guys:

How are your friendships with guys different than your friendships with girls?

E.J. Y.: "I feel more comfortable around guys. I can tell them more than I can tell girls."

Drew W.: "My friendships with males are a little more real. When I'm with girls, sometimes it's hard not to try to impress them."

Chris J.: "With my guy friends, I talk about sports and girls. But with girls, it's harder to express my feelings."

Jonathan M.: "For me, they're pretty much the same. The major difference is that with a girl, I might hold the door open for her, tone down my language, and really listen to her."

Brandon W.: "With guys, I feel absolutely comfortable talking about almost everything."

Michael K.: "I can say things to guys that I wouldn't normally say to girls. Girls are usually more sensitive about stuff."

Kevin C.: "With guys, you can be more open about your feelings. With girls, it's easy for them to take something the wrong way."

mirror mirror

by Kara Powell and Kendall Payne

COMPARISON

COMPARISON

*WHAT MICHELLE PFEIFFER DOESN'T WANT YOU TO KNOW
Does She Have it All?

* CONFESSIONS
A Beauty and an Ordinary Reveal

* POLITICS
Powder Room vs. the Whitehouse

Plus: Try our Mirror, Mirror Quiz

What Michelle Pfeiffer Doesn't Want You to Know

Most guys I know think Michelle Pfeiffer is pretty hot. She can go from baseball-hat-wearing-cute to way-sexy in seconds. It would take about a million plastic surgeries to make me look like her (sigh).

I saw a cover of an Esquire magazine with her picture on it. It said, "What Michelle Pfeiffer Needs is Absolutely Nothing." She looked gorgeous. She was wearing this red dress and had her head tipped back with her mouth open in this huge (and of course sexy) smile. The magazine came out in 1990 and I still remember the picture.

I also remember the day I received a copy of the bill from a friend of a friend of a friend (of a friend of a friend…) of the photographer who not only took that picture, but then touched it up. Here are the touch-ups listed on the bill:

"Clean up complexion, soften eye lines, soften smile line, add color to lips, trim chin, remove neck lines, soften line under ear lobe, add highlights to earrings, add blush to cheek, clean up neck line, remove stray hair, remove hair strands on dress, adjust color and add hair on top of head, add dress on side to create better line, add dress on shoulder, clean up and smooth dress folds under arm and create one seam on image of right side, add forehead to create better line, remove red dress at corner of neck, add dress on shoulder to sharpen and create a better line, soften neck muscle a bit, and soften neck line on image on left side."

(My personal favorite is that they added forehead. That's gotta hurt!)

No wonder I get bummed that I don't look like Michelle Pfeiffer in the picture. I'm not sure Michelle Pfeiffer looks that way!

The Comparison Game

Whenever I play the comparison game with Michelle Pfeiffer, or anyone else for that matter, I've got to remember that…

* Even those who are "beautiful" wish they could be like others. Want proof? Read the real life confessions of Kathleen and Jamie on page 62.

* There's no way I'll ever win at the comparison game. There's always someone who is a little bit more talented, confident, or pretty than me.

* Even if you could win, you'd be focusing on the wrong thing. Your mom's been telling you for years that it's your heart that really matters, (and for years you've been blowing her off). But that whole "heart mattering most" idea wasn't hers. It started 3,000 years ago, and get this, it was first said not about a girl, but about a guy who ended up being a king. So maybe the advice isn't so bad after all. See "Simone's Story" on page 64 for the full story.

✳ Mirrors

By Charlotte Cooper, 18, from a suburb in the West
Taken from Sara Shandler, Ophelia Speaks (New York: Harper Perennial, 1999), 7.

I often hear,
Mostly from psychologists on talk shows,
How teenagers see distorted images in our full-length mirrors.
The ones that set decorators in movies and on television,
Border with Prom pictures, snapshots and
Cute boys: Ben Affleck, Matt Damon, David Duchovny, David Boreanaz.
In my room, Ben and Matt and both Davids are next to my bed.
They are on the wall across from the mirror.
On my desk
On my ceiling.
But not around my mirror.
Around my mirror are women:
Nadia Anerman, Kate Moss, Amber Valleta, Shalom Harlow.
I get to see them as I look at myself.
They are my goals. They are my aspirations.
And then I wonder why I hate myself.
When I am alone in my room, I look at myself
And I am disgusted.
After seeing what I should look like around my mirror,
I hate my body and self.
I truly believe that I should look that way,
Because no matter what I say in class about images,
I truly believe that it is my own fault that I don't look like a model.

Powder Room Politics

Sometimes the girls' powder room (bathroom) is more politically charged than the White House. OK, maybe that's an overstatement, but see if you can relate to these lyrics from the song "Powder Room Politics" by Sam Phillips (the artist formerly known as Leslie Phillips).

Well, I walk inside just to fix my hair
And the girls at the mirror all start to stare
They look back at their reflection and we all compare
And it's powder room politics

While I wish I could wear this one girl's size
Another girl was wishing that she had my eyes
And we were all feeling worthless until I realized
It's just powder room politics

Oh, well, we feel like we're not worth much in any scene
If we don't look like the girls in magazines
And we're all being robbed of our self-esteem

Well, I told that girl that she had nice eyes
And then I stopped worrying about my size
And as I left, I was glad to leave the lies
Of powder room politics

Think about it...

✳ What does Phillips mean by "powder room politics?"

✳ How have you experienced powder room politics, if at all?

✳ Is it better, worse, or the same at church than at school? Explain. The girl in the song seems to make a change at the end. Describe that change.

✳ What thoughts or attitudes generally bring about that change?

✳ What would it take for you to move beyond and be set free from powder room politics?

✳ What one thing can you do today to move toward breaking free from powder room politics?

Confessions of a Beauty
By Leslie

I know other girls wish they looked like me. They've told me so. Blonde hair, blue eyes, acne-free skin and straight teeth. It's nothing I've done to myself. It's just how I am.

What they don't know is that I wish I was different. When people look at me, they just see a pretty face. They don't see what's inside the "package". They just "ooh" and "ahh" at the wrapping.

Especially guys. When a guy likes me, I never know if it's because of the real me, or the outside me. Most guys like me before they even talk to me, so I guess it's just my looks they like.

So I guess I wish my skin wasn't so clear and my eyes weren't so blue. I guess I wish I looked a little more normal. A little more like everyone else.

Confessions of an Ordinary
By Kathleen

Ever been to Wal-Mart? That should be my nickname. I'm Wal-Mart living in a Saks Fifth Avenue world.

All my friends are prettier than me. Michelle is tan all year round. I go to Hawaii for a week and come back the same color as when I left. She could take the trash out and walk in darker!

Dolores has perfect hair. Perfect. When I spend the night at her house, my hair is tornado city. But she wakes up and her hair looks all cute.

Leslie's got a body to die for. Like seriously, all the guys talk about her. The girls too. Summer's the worst. I don't even go to the beach with her anymore. She's the gorgeous princess. I'm the ugly duckling. I'd give anything to look like her.

Real Guys...

We invited them to read the "Confessions of an 'Ordinary'" and "Confessions of a 'Beauty'" that you have already read. Then we asked them a few more questions to get a guy's perspective.

What would you say to Kathleen, if you had the chance?

Drew W.: "It isn't the outside that always matters. A kind heart can get you a long way."

Jonathan M.: "If a guy doesn't like you because of your looks then he isn't worth your time. A real man looks at personality."

Michael K.: "I guess it's kind of natural to think that you wish you had better teeth or were skinnier. I do the same thing. But I try to say to myself, 'It's what's inside that counts.' You probably think it's only beauty that guys look at. But guys are attracted to personalities too. "

Kevin C.: "Guys feel the same way. There are always the cute guys, the built guys, and then there's the rest of us. Guys will fall in love with you for what's inside. And when they love you, they will see you as beautiful, no matter what you think."

Brandon W.: "I know that girls struggle a lot with their outward appearance, but people who are comfortable with themselves are more attractive. If you make your personality more important than your appearance, you will be much happier with yourself and people will find you more attractive."

How about Leslie? What would you say to her?

Drew W.: "You were blessed with beauty. Find a guy who respects your heart as much as your body."

Jonathan M.: "Don't be so judgmental. Maybe a guy really does like the real you, and not just how you look."

E.J.: "You sound like a nice person. Maybe that's why people like you."

Kevin C.: "Eventually you'll find a guy who loves you for what's inside. Be patient. There really are caring guys out there."

Brandon W.: "What you need to do is just talk to people and show them your insides. Ignore those who are only interested in your appearance."

What does this tell you about how girls feel about themselves?

Jonathan M.: "Girls are pretty insecure. I guess I knew that already, but Kathleen and Leslie show me how insecure they really are. But looks aren't the only thing that matter to guys."

Drew W.: "No matter how girls look or act, they're always going to compare themselves with others and feel like they come up short."

E.J.: "Girls like to judge themselves. They're never happy with themselves. I wish that would change."

Simone Says

You've heard the old saying, "You can't judge a book by its cover," probably 42,000 times. And of those 42,000 times, you've probably blown it off 41,999 times. But maybe this one time as you read Simone's story, you'll think about it a second longer, and maybe it will sink in a millimeter deeper.

Simone couldn't believe his luck. When he signed up for the two-week university swim camp, he knew the morning and afternoon workouts would be excruciatingly tough, and that 6 am weight-lifting would pretty much stink, no surprises. But he had no idea the night life would be as good as it was. And Simone lived for the nightlife.

Of the 113 high school juniors and seniors who signed up for camp, 32 were guys. Do the math. That means 81 were girls. That's like 2.5 girls for every guy.

Simone was tired of the girls at his school. They were all so fake. He wanted his crack at his 2.5 girls.

And these 81 girls were good looking. Swimming does a body good. Makes the waist small and the legs lean. Bleaches your hair and gives you a tan. At night, Simone felt like he was hanging out with candidates for a Miss Teen USA pageant or something.

By Tuesday, Simone knew his search was over. That morning was his turn for his backstroke to be filmed underwater. While he was waiting for the camera to be set up, shivering because of the cold cement around the pool, a leggy blonde came up to him and asked,

"Is this where we wait to be filmed?"

You can wait anywhere you want to, Simone thought.

Instead he said,

"Yeah, I think. What's your name?"

"Desiree."

Desiree. Like Desire. And that Simone did. Desiree had this beaming smile and deep blue eyes. Simone asked,

"Desiree, wanna grab some coffee tonight after dinner?"

"Sure, meet me out front of the cafeteria at 8."

The first 20 minutes of their date went pretty well. Desiree was really easy to talk to. There was no lull in the conversation or anything.

Soon Simone realized why. Desiree never stopped talking. No wonder she had such a great smile. She used her jaw so much she had all sorts of practice.

As Simone walked Desiree back to her dorm, she said, "Maybe we could do this again sometime."

Simone, avoiding eye contact, mumbled, "Yeah, sure." Only if your mouth is wired shut, he thought.

Back to the drawing board. One down and 80 more to go.

Continued on next page...

By Friday, he was getting a bit desperate. Lots of the other guys were already hooking up. The field was getting smaller. Camp was half over. Simone needed to act fast.

Little did he know that Carmela was way ahead of him. She had spotted Simone the first day. Though bummed that he had taken Desiree out, she never saw the two together, and that gave her hope. Maybe if she got in the dinner line right after him, they'd have four or five minutes to chat as they went through the line, and they might even end up at the same table.

So that night, Simone found himself standing in line, talking to a really nice girl who said her name was Carmela. Since he didn't see any of his friends in the dining area, he figured he might as well sit with her.

She was a much better listener than Desiree. And most other girls for that matter. After they finished their veggie lasagna, he asked, "Hey Carmela, wanna grab some ice cream?" And a few minutes later they were on their way to the campus center to grab some mint and chip.

On their way back, they passed a few other kids from the camp. Carmela gave a "what's up?", a big hug and a smile to one of the girls named Danae. After a few moments of small talk, Carmela and Simone moved on with a wave and a smile.

"I hate her," Carmela whispered after they were out of earshot. "She thinks she's so cool, but she's really just a poor girl from the Northwest part of town."

And that opened the floodgates. Carmela begin gushing with criticism of all the other girls at the camp. OK, not all the girls, only about 20 of them. But to Simone, 20 was enough. No way did he want to hang with someone who was so petty. It'd only be a matter of time until he ended up on her black list.

Three days left and counting. Simone had already met most of the girls, and hadn't clicked with any of them. That afternoon, he was assigned to a different lane for practice, from lane 3 to lane 4.

The six girls who usually swam in lane 4 had kind of kept to themselves. Simone only knew two of their names. When the freestyle set ended, he introduced himself to the other four: Candice, Kimberly, Kristi, and Angela. Nice girls, he thought.

These nice girls had made some enemies, though. Some of the girls in lane 3 thought they were snobby since they didn't talk to others very much. Two of the lane 3 girls even stole Candice's goggles when she was swimming the 400. When she finished, Candice reached around on the deck for her goggles but couldn't find them. She knew from the giggling of the girls in lane 3 that somehow they were involved.

Simone thought Candice would blow up at them. Or maybe just ignore them and try to finish her workout without them. But instead she said,

"Hey, can I please have my goggles back? I can tell by the way you're laughing and staring at me that you've got them. And since I assume you're a bit more mature than the average seven year-old, I'm sure you'll give them back to me."

The lane 3 girls weren't laughing anymore. One of them was silent, desperately trying to come up with a come back that was better than,

"Oh yeah."

Continued on next page …

The other one kicked over and gave Candice her goggles, muttering, "Sorry," as she turned and kicked away.

Simone was impressed. Candice had zinged them, but wasn't mean about it. She didn't go running to the coach. She figured out what to do herself.

While Candice wasn't quite as blonde as muscular as the other girls, she was still pretty nice to look at. And she actually looked better right now to Simone than she had before. Maybe he'd see if she was free for a fruit smoothie after practice.

The names and details of this story have been changed to protect the innocent.

OK, not exactly to protect the innocent, but to give you a new twist on an old story. How old? 3,000 years to be exact. And it wasn't about finding a girlfriend, but finding a king.

Simone = Samuel

Samuel was a prophet searching for the right new king. Simone wanted to find the right girl. Both could not afford to make their decision based on outward appearance alone.

Desiree and/or Carmela = King Saul

Saul was quite a looker (King Saul in the Old Testament— not Saul who became the apostle Paul in the New Testament). Saul started out a pretty good King of Israel, but his disobedience to God and behavior soon betrayed his impure heart and showed he lacked inner character. So Samuel had to find a new king. Similarly, Desiree and Carmela looked good at first, but as Simone got to know them, their behavior showed him their hearts weren't so pretty.

Candice = David

Just like with Candice, David's "heart" took a little longer for Samuel to notice. While Saul stood out because of his appearance, David stood out for different reasons. He stood out for what was inside of him.

In 1 Samuel 16:1-13, God told Samuel that the new king would be one of the sons of Jesse, but the first seven sons didn't fit the bill. Then Jesse called in David, the youngest of the eight boys.

Now David was pretty good looking. The Bible even calls him "fine." But David had something else going for him. Zoom in on 1 Samuel 16:7. The Lord tells Samuel, "The Lord does not look at the things man looks at. Man looks at the outward appearance, but the Lord looks at the heart."

The word "heart" doesn't just mean that red organ in your chest that pumps blood. In Hebrew (the language it was first written in), it means the center of your moral, spiritual, and intellectual life. Bottom line: it means the real you.

God looks past the outer wrapping paper to the real you inside. Maybe instead of comparing our hair, eyes, and body to everybody else's, we should spend a bit more energy fixing up our insides.

For more information on how to do this, see every other article in this whole chapter.

At first glance...

Your favorite aunt Lynda from Chicago has come to visit you. She's lugged in two gifts: one for you and one for your sister. You're the oldest, so you get to choose first. Your sister gets the other gift. Which would you choose, Box 1 or Box 2?

A second look...

Think about the boxes. Imagine that part of the paper has been ripped and you can see what lies beneath the wrapping. Box 1 contains a box of crayons. Box 2 contains a stereo. Now which box would you choose?

If you're like 99% of the population, you'd first choose Box 1 because it looks better, but then you'd choose Box 2 because only a fool would choose crayons over a stereo.

Did you know...

* There are 3 billion women who don't look like supermodels and only 8 who do!

* Marilyn Monroe wore a size 12.

* If Barbie were a real woman, she'd have to walk on all fours due to her proportions.

* The average American woman weighs 144 pounds and wears between a size 12 and 14.

* Twenty years ago, models weighed an average of 8% less than the average woman. Now they wear 23% less than the average woman.

* I REMEMBER

By Kendall

I remember… when I didn't want to go to ballet class anymore because I didn't like looking at myself in a leotard.

I remember…not wanting to wear tank-tops or sleeveless dresses because I didn't like the way my arms looked in them.

I remember…lying in bed at night, wishing for a pill that would make me skinny as I slept so that I could go to school the next day and all the boys would like me.

I remember…writing a contract for myself that said, "If I lose 30 pounds, I will buy $100 worth of new clothes." I even signed it.

I remember…really liking bagels with peanut butter on them… lots of peanut butter.

I remember…sneaking food out of the kitchen after dinner was over, hoping no one saw me.

I remember…when kids at school would say the word, "fat," my heart would start pounding because I was afraid they were talking about me.

And, I remember…sitting in a radio station after my album came out. I was talking to the dj about one of my songs called "supermodels." It's a funny song about girls, insecurities, and the fact that we "hate" supermodels. Then he said something that basically changed my life. He said, "I have never met a woman who is happy with herself." I thought about that for a moment and then it hit me, neither had I.

* Imperfect? Join the Crowd

Everyone who I think is perfect sees all their own flaws and thinks someone else is perfect. I had never met a woman who loves herself completely without wanting to change a thing.

I remember thinking, can this be true? Is this just a sick cycle that never stops repeating itself? If I lose 15 pounds, will I finally be happy with myself, or will I find something else that needs to change? When will it ever stop? Who's going to finally stand up and say, "THAT'S IT! NO MORE!"

Then I began to notice the different body frames around me. I'd walk through airports and watch people. I noticed tall people and short people. Some had broad shoulders and skinny hips. Some had skinny shoulders and broad hips. Some had bad skin, but great figures. Some had about 75 "extra" pounds, disbursed among their butts and thighs and arms and sometimes ankles and wrists, but had the prettiest faces.

I noticed the way men look at women, and which ones they look at, and how they look at me. I noticed spare tires, huge breasts, balding heads, tight pants, fat fingers. And I noticed myself in every reflection I could find, which is something I do all the time. Call it obsessive. Call it stupid. Nonetheless, it's a part of my everyday existence.

* When Comparison Comes Between Us

So here's the question. With so many shapes and sizes in the world, both male and female, why do we try to all look the same? Why do I want to look one way when God obviously made me different? And with that
Continued on next page…

simple thought I decided, it stops here. I am going to be the first woman who loves everything about myself. Since there is only one of me in this entire world, I may as well concentrate on being her and stop trying to be someone else.

At a church barbecue, I saw a small group of little girls playing under the spray of the sprinklers. One was lean and thin with long legs and tan in her itsy-bitsy bikini. Another was short with thick little legs, a round tummy and kind of a pasty, white color. They were both playing a game very intensely. Nothing mattered but the game. They weren't wondering if anyone was watching them. When the boys came up, they acted like they had been acting before. They talked like normal and the goal was still to have as much fun as possible.

I sat and watched them play for a long time...and then I started to cry. I started thinking that one day the shorter, stout girl will secretly dislike this other girl for being skinnier. It won't happen all at once, but there will come a time when she won't want to stand next to her in a bathing suit. "Friend" will become "enemy." I wanted to grab her and shake her by both of her arms and say, "Don't grow up! At least not into that. Stay in the happy place where you're not afraid to wear a bathing suit and play your hardest."

Then I looked at the other girl and I began to cry for her also. I was sad that she might not ever find out what she really has to offer because she is so beautiful and perfect. Then I wanted to grab her and shake her and say, "Don't you ever think you're better than anyone simply because you're cute."

You Were Born to Be an Original

There's a verse in the Bible that says, "Before I formed you in the womb I knew you" (Jeremiah 1:5). God is very clear that he made us and that he knew us even then. He made us with a specific plan in mind.

Sometimes it's hard to think that when we feel different. Sometimes we just wish we could look like everyone else, but think how boring that would be if everyone looked the same. A bunch of copies when we're all supposed to be a bunch of originals. We honor God most when we learn to appreciate and grow in love for the unique individual he made us to be.

It's silly really, to want to look like someone else. Imagine if other things around your house wanted to look different. What if your refrigerator wanted to look like your telephone? You couldn't really store that much food in it, now could you? What if your sofa wanted to switch places with your TV set? Ouch!

What if animals wanted to be different shapes and sizes? What if your dog sat around all day saying, "Oh, if only I looked like a cat." Or if a mouse spent its whole life wishing it had a long neck like a giraffe. These comparisons seem crazy, but then why do we compare ourselves to other people? Whenever we do that, we always come up short.

But, Maybe Comparison Isn't So Bad After All...

OK, I'm starting to think that maybe comparison has gotten a bad rap. It's not its fault that we've done it so poorly.

The real problem isn't that we compare. The real problem is WHAT we compare.

It's like a recipe. Say you're trying to make chocolate chip cookies. You're using your grandma's cookbook, and it's so old that some pages are missing. So you follow the first half of the recipe with no problems.

Continued on next page...

Then when you look at the next page, you're a bit surprised that it calls for tomato sauce and olives. But hey, you've got to follow the recipe, right?

15 minutes and 375 degrees later, what you have is guaranteed-to-make-you-vomit hockey pucks. No one will eat them, not even your dog.

The next time you try chocolate chip cookies, you decide to use the recipe on the chocolate chip bag. Flour, brown sugar, butter, salt, vanilla, eggs. This time it makes a lot more sense to you. You end up with golden mouth-watering cookies that even your picky step-brother likes.

What's the difference? The ingredients. No matter how long you mix or bake them, tomato sauce and olives are a far cry from butter and sugar.

The same is true with comparison. It's not the process of comparison that is evil. It's what we put into our brain that we decide to compare that can end up smelling pretty rank.

So if I compare my body to Heather's, and my legs to Kathleen's, and my nose to Junia's, I'll probably end up wanting to paste a "loser" label across my forehead.

✳ Comparison Good?

I could think about how nice Chrissy is to her neighbors and think, Wow, I need to spend time helping others like Chrissy.

I could think about how Kim does a good job spending time with her parents and think, Hmmm… Maybe I should try that too.

Is that really so bad? Well, if I become obsessed with the inner beauty of others, maybe. But if I just look around and learn from them, and am challenged to be all that I can be by comparing myself to some part of them, then maybe I will become a better person. And as I become a better person, maybe they start learning from me. And pretty soon we have a big circle of people pointing at each other and saying, "You made me a better person."

Mirror Mirror

Do this: Take the following 2 quizzes, putting a check mark in the box that best describes how often you do the following.

Quiz 1: Skin Deep

How often do you do each of the following...	0 Never	1 Once in a while	2 Lots	3 All the time
Hop in your friend's parents' car and think it's nicer than your parents' car				
Visit a friend's room and think, "I wish I had that stereo/ TV/ computer/ closet..." whatever				
Check out another girl's outfit and wish you had it.				
Wish you had a friend's hair instead of your own.				
Want to trade make-up with a friend.				
Wish guys liked you like they like your friend.				
Want to learn to flirt and tease guys like other girls.				

Add up your scores to find out how you rate.

0-7 You're Confident.
Sure, you look around and can't help think that others have better or nicer stuff than you, but it doesn't get you down. You know who you are and you're pretty happy with it. Take a minute to thank God for the self-confidence He's given you.

8-15 You're In Between.
You're like a lot of girls: you compare yourself with others but you're not obsessed with how others look. Your outlook on yourself and your life would improve if you became increasingly grateful to God for how He has made you and what He has given you. Make a list of 3 things about your body that you really like, and thank God for them right now.

16-24 You're Surfacey.
"If only..." is one of your constant cries. "If only you had that hair...," "If only I had that lipstick...," "If only he liked me back...". Focus more on developing inner qualities than on the outside. Outside stuff doesn't last. Put down the mirror and bring out the magnifying glass to look a little closer at who you are inside. Ask God to help you be grateful for what you have and how you look. Refuse to envy others. Think of 2 things you wish you could change about how you look, and thank God for them. For example, say your eyes are deep brown instead of muddy hazel. Then consider, what if God hadn't given you eyes? No teeth? Focus on celebrating what you do have. And thank God for it.

Now do this. **Now take the second quiz and see how you rate.**

✳ Quiz 2: Heart Chart

How often do you do the following?	0 Never	1 Once in a while	2 Lots	3 All the time
See someone being nice to the new girl and wishing you had done it.				
Want to be like your friend who changes the subject when it gets gossipy.				
Want to be like the friend who always seems to be willing (and has time) to help others.				
Wish you could be like your friend, who always cheers up others when they're bummed.				
Want to be like another girl who's a Christian at your school and doesn't seem to give in as much as you do.				
Wish you could laugh at yourself and some of the dorky things you do like your friend laughs at herself.				
Wish you could be like your friend, who doesn't spread a rumor even when it's a juicy one.				

How do you rate?

0-7 You've got a great heart and inner qualities, or... you don't care enough about inner qualities

Re-read the 7 questions in Quiz 2 and pick out two statements that you most want to develop in your life. Ask God to develop those parts of your heart this week

8-15 You're medium.

On the one hand, you're pretty OK with who you are on the inside, but on the other hand, you know you need to grow. That's a pretty good place to be. Thank God for 2 qualities about your heart that you really like, and then ask Him to make you even more kind and thoughtful this week.

16-24 You're Envious.

You've gone a bit too far in wanting to be like other people. You probably get down on yourself a lot and think you're not a very good person. Sure, there are parts of you that aren't so good, but there are probably some really beautiful parts inside of you also that you need to focus on and celebrate more. Make a list of 5 nice things you've done for others in the last week. Next to each thing, write down one thing that shows about your heart. For example, you helped your brother with his math homework rather than talk to a friend on the phone. That shows that you are willing to sacrifice for others. Got it? Good. Now get to it.

Think about it...

* *What's the difference between the two quizzes?*

* *Which quiz did you score more points on? What does that tell you about yourself?*

* *Lots of girls score higher on Quiz 1 than Quiz 2. Any ideas on why that might be?*

* *Imagine if the girls at your school, or your church for that matter, spent more time trying to learn inner beauty from their friends instead of wishing they had someone else's outer beauty. How would your school or church be different?*

* *Imagine you spent more time focusing on inner beauty than outer beauty, how would your schedule be different? How would it change how you felt about yourself? Why?*

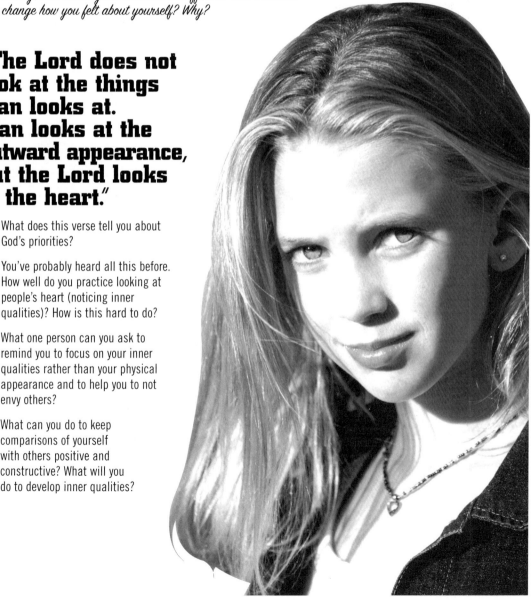

"The Lord does not look at the things man looks at. Man looks at the outward appearance, but the Lord looks at the heart."

* What does this verse tell you about God's priorities?

* You've probably heard all this before. How well do you practice looking at people's heart (noticing inner qualities)? How is this hard to do?

* What one person can you ask to remind you to focus on your inner qualities rather than your physical appearance and to help you to not envy others?

* What can you do to keep comparisons of yourself with others positive and constructive? What will you do to develop inner qualities?

Supermodels.

By Kendall

What a strange thing that we refer to women and men who happen to be a certain weight or a certain look as "models." Lets scratch just an inch below that surface. A "model" is defined as "an exemplary person or thing, ideal." Hmmm.

We have model citizens who show us how to serve our country. We have model students who show us how to study and learn. And we have supermodels...who are supposed to show us how to look?

If so, that seems pretty strange, because female models are mostly 5'10" and above, when most American women are 5'4" to 5'5"—which cannot be helped. I mean yeah, you can starve yourself to the point of reaching 100 lbs. But you can't stretch your bones 5 inches.

Then it also seems strange to me that a model has a certain facial construction...which is pretty much perfect. Now, unless I missed a meeting, I never remember being asked how I wanted my face to be configured. Oh no, no, no this nose is far too high on my face. And this upper lip is far too small. It needs to look swollen.

To be a model would imply there is a standard this person has reached. And it would also infer that others, with hard work and determination, could also achieve the same lofty and exalted position. However, this is simply impossible. And I think every time we call someone a supermodel, we somehow take a blow to our own originality.

So me and my best friend "B" were sitting on a park bench. And she was just not having a good day (as girls tend to do every once in a while). I was trying to encourage her and re-remind her of all the inward qualities that really matter in life. I told her,

"It's your heart that counts, your personality, and your character! And any man would be crazy not to love you!"
I really meant it! She's an absolutely amazing girl. But she looked at me, on the verge of tears and says,
"But I feel fat."
As I consoled her, we started gaining confidence. We told ourselves, as it was our normal custom to do,
"I like me!"
And she'd look at me and say, "I like you too!" And vice versa. And then I'd say,
"We are beautiful women."
"Yeah", she'd chime in.
"Who love God!"
"Yeah!"
She'd wrinkle her forehead and start nodding in support.
"And one day, some guy is going to think we're amazing! and
love us... just as we are!"
"YEAH!"

We could feel reality rushing back to our heads and our pity
party was being washed away. And then it happened...right at
the pinnacle moment, right at the top of the roller coaster, as
you're picking up steam, about to go over the top...the ride
stops.

Our attention was captivated by the most beautiful, perfect
looking woman we had both ever seen in our entire lives. It
seemed as if she was floating by. She looked like Faith Hill, only better.

She had gorgeous, long blonde hair. She wore white, sleeveless summer dress (perfect arms by the way, no visible
flab what so ever). Amazing skin. No makeup and looked gorgeous. And to top it off she was like 8 months pregnant—one of those women who only looks pregnant when you see her silhouette. When you look at them from
behind, or even straight on, you can't tell they're pregnant. (I "hate" them!!!)

In total, it probably took her 15 seconds to walk by. But the impression she left us with will last a lifetime. B
looked at me, with her jaw dropped, and just shook her head back and forth. Every insecurity we had so nicely
tucked into bed was awake inside and screaming. Why did she have to walk by right then?

I have now lived many more moments where the "lady in the white dress" has crossed my path. It never gets any
easier. She, or someone like her, seems to always be there just when I'm feeling pretty secure. It's like she just
wants to stop by and rub it in. But I got the ultimate "revenge."

I wrote a song about that moment. I called it supermodels. And one of the greatest thrills of my songwriting career
is to see girls' faces in the audience when I sing that song. Or to hear their stories of the confidence it inspires in
them. One girl told me that she and her friends make hot fudge sundaes and turn my song up really loud—and eat
until they want to pass out! That makes me happy. And it makes B happy too.

*Real Girls
Tough situations for you to grapple with...

Don't you hate it when you get caught in the middle of things? Like when your friend asks you a really hard question and you don't know what to say? It's especially hard when friends are comparing themselves to other people—or one another.

We asked our real girls what they would say in the two tough spot situations below. You'd better read carefully. If this stuff hasn't happened to you, it will soon.

Marissa's No Fun Day

Your friend, Marissa, likes Steve. Steve's friend, Jason, tells Marissa that Steve thinks Hallie is more fun than she is. Marissa calls you on the phone to tell you. She's crying so hard you can hardly understand what she says. "Is Hallie really more fun than me?"

What would you say?

Emily B.: "If Steve is going to be the kind of guy who's always comparing you to other girls, are you really going to be happy in that kind of relationship? Don't settle for him."

Brittany H.: "I'd probably try to logically figure it out with her. I'd find out what kind of girl Steve likes (sporty, prissy, etc.) and find the differences between Hallie and Marissa."

Christy G.: "I'd tell her that if Steve thinks that Hallie is better than she is, then he doesn't know what he's talking about. She can do better than Steve. I'd also encourage her and talk about all of the things she has going for her."

Nicole R.: "I would say, 'Yeah, right, who cares?' because I HATE it when girls let guys make them feel bad. Boyfriends are way overrated anyway."

Searcy C.: "I'd probably tell her that Steve isn't worth the tears. In the big scheme of things, he doesn't matter. I would comfort her but nicely tell her to 'get over it.'"

Elaine W.: "You both are fun. Don't let it get you down. If Steve doesn't see how cool you are then he doesn't deserve you anyway."

Erica M.: "You're perfect the way you are. There's more to you than just being fun. If Steve doesn't want to see who you really are, then he doesn't want you enough."

Julia's Complaints

Julia is a complainer. No matter where she is, and who she's with, she always complains about what she has. "I wish I lived in your house, Samantha." "Angel, your clothes are so much better than mine." "Brianna, I wish I could trade lipsticks with you. Mine is so-last-year."

You're starting to get tired of Julia's whining, and so you're avoiding her at school. She stops you after third period and asks you what's up.

What do you tell her?

Erica M.: "I'd tell Julia that she needs to appreciate what she has. She complains too much over things that aren't worth complaining over. If she doesn't have it, then she should pray about it. If she gets it, then it was meant to be. If not, forget about it."

Macall R.: "I really like being your friend, but I think you're a little hard on yourself. You and your personality are great, so you should be happy with that."

Kathy W.: "Honestly, I would probably tell her I just had a lot of stuff on my mind. I wouldn't confront her about it until I absolutely felt I had to."

Elaine W.: "Don't take this the wrong way, Julia, but sometimes you compare yourself with other people too much. You don't even realize all you do have."

Searcy C.: "I would probably tell her that it annoys me when she is constantly unsatisfied with what she has. There are lots of people who are satisfied with practically nothing."

Emily C.: "I would probably make up some excuse, because I wouldn't want to be mean or confront her. I would try to come up with something that was at least a little true, like I've been busy with other stuff."

Emily B.: "I would tell her the truth about how I feel and let her know that if she's not satisfied with what she has now, she probably won't EVER be satisfied."

mirror mirror

by Kara Powell and Kendall Payne

mixed messages

* **I AM WOMAN**
  Hear Me Whimper

* **LEADERSHIP**
  The Gentle Strength

* **YOUR BODY**
  Weapon or Enemy

* **Plus: The Journal of a 10th Grade Girl**

I Am Woman, Hear Me…Whimper?

Lots of what I learned about being a girl came from "The Love Boat." Well, not really lots, but at least one thing. I learned that girls and women have to deal with some major mixed messages.

If you don't watch Nick at Nite, you've probably never seen the old show, "The Love Boat." Basically, in each show, the ship's crew begins by welcoming a handful of new characters on board. During the cruise, a regular soap opera would unfold. She liked him, but he didn't like her. Or a middle-aged couple couldn't figure out how to get their fifteen year-old daughter to talk to them, but she had no problem talking to Captain Steubing. And on it went. 53 minutes of relationship roller coasters.

In one episode, a brilliant and beautiful astronomer came on board. She had two goals: to relax, and to find a guy. One of her friends advised her, "Your problem is that you're too smart. You've got to dumb it down a bit in order to catch a guy."

Desperate to get a guy, she followed her friend's advice. And it worked. The dumber she acted, the more that men liked her.

There was one particular guy who was more decent than the rest and who liked her a lot. One problem, though. As he explained one late night as they were standing by the boat railing with the moon reflecting on the ocean, "You're just not smart enough for me."

That did it. She pointed up at the moon and asked, "Would you like me to tell you something about the moon?" And then the floodgates opened, "The moon is 3,476 kilometers in diameter and is located approximately 385,400 kilometers from the earth."

The guy couldn't believe it. She was smarter than him. At the end of the cruise (and the episode), they walked off the boat arm-in-arm, on their way to what was sure to be a rosy romance.

Love yourself…but be somebody else!

So is it a good idea for you to hide who you are for awhile like the astronomer did? Certainly OK if that's the only way you'll ever date someone, right? Hmmm. Girls get mixed messages, love yourself—but change everything about yourself as necessary to get guys.

Another area where girls and women get mixed messages is in the area of leadership. It's OK to lead and be strong—but don't be too strong since so many male leaders perceive strong women to be threatening.

You may have heard in your History class that in China from the tenth century until the twentieth century, women's feet were made "more dainty and ladylike" by being painfully stuffed into tiny shoes that would stunt the growth of their feet. They couldn't be too big or they might scare away men. We've come a long way, but maybe not as far as we thought.

At times, we females feel like big strong eagles. We know ourselves, we stretch out our wings, we look to the sky, ready to fly. But then we're told that we'd better clip our wings a bit — wouldn't want to create too much wind or anything. Love yourself, you're an eagle…but try to be a canary.

The Truth Will Set You Free

I've raised just two examples of mixed messages, but here are some others you might be getting from our culture:

* *Be nice but not too nice.*
* *Be sexy but not too sexy.*
* *State your ideas, but don't be too loud.*
* *Love your body, but change everything about it.*

And on and on it goes...

We think there's a way to be the eagle you're meant to be in the midst of a culture that tries to make you a canary. This chapter swirls around two hopes.

1. Your eyes will be opened. Lots of girls don't realize the mixed messages that they're immersed in, or even spreading themselves. You can't stop something until you identify what that something is.

2. Your mind will be filled. Knowledge is power, and knowing practical ways to respond to the mixed messages that you're swimming through is the best way to make it to the finish line.

My Mixed Message

By Kendall

I've got a mixed message for you…I love the idea of this book, but during the writing, I often wondered if I should be writing for it! No one at Youth Specialties (the publisher) wants to hear that. Kara, my partner in crime on this project, doesn't want to hear that. Heck, even I don't want to say it! But it's reality.

As I've been writing these pages I've become increasingly aware that I am in no way qualified to instruct you. I still really struggle with insecurities. I mean, if I wanted to ask someone about marriage I would probably seek out someone who has 30, 40 or even 50 years under their belt—I probably wouldn't ask someone who's been divorced 3 or 4 times. Same with parenting, I would ask advice from parents who raised decent kids, not the parents of criminals of our society. So I ask myself, what do I have to say to you?

We're probably close in age. I'm twenty-two.

We probably watch the same movies and TV programs.

Our high schools are probably pretty similar. My high school had a popular group, and an unpopular group (which of course I was a part of)…how about you?

I fight feelings every day of low self esteem.

I fight every day with the world of food. Which ones are good for me, which ones don't like me, and which ones I like more than I should (namely chocolate). We are probably a lot more alike than either of us realize.

I compare myself to every other girl I meet. How about you? (By the way, if you don't do that yet… don't ever start.) If I'm standing next to a woman who looks great in her jeans and I don't, I somehow feel less than her, which is insane.

It's not only insane because it tortures me unjustly, but it's also insane because in this world there are two types of humans, boys and girls. Most boys are very confusing…and so the only thing we have left is the sisterhood. But that provides no comfort because we are all sizing each other up and, many times, tearing one another down.

My boyfriend is constantly reminding me to be nice to other girls. I tell him I feel threatened, but he doesn't understand. And ultimately I don't understand.

The other day I had a melt down because I wanted to buy new clothes. Unfortunately, I can't afford the clothes I want. I had to go to a birthday party and if you've ever tried to get dressed when you, as we women say it, "don't have a thing to wear" you know its not a safe or stable time. My poor boyfriend was trying to be so sensitive but I was acting like a fire-breathing dragon. And I couldn't stop myself from freaking out no matter how hard I tried. I ended up in my bathroom crying until I felt a little better.

So that's my mixed message. I want to teach you something wise, but I am still so foolish. I want to inspire you to be free but I still wear my chains like jewelry. But hopefully my honesty and vulnerability speaks louder than my false confidence. I want you to know that fame, fortune and popularity never bring security. That self confidence is only found in knowing that your Abba Father truly loves you. That is the only way we are ever secure in our skin, knowing our "Daddy" loves us, just as we are, and that makes us OK.

The Journal of a 10th grade girl...

By Sara Williams, October 12, 2001

Dear God,

It's 3:40PM and I just got home from school. All I can say is that today was a weird day! Classes were OK and my test in history went fine, but after lunch I had this random conversation that made me kind of mad. Random conversations don't normally faze me, but today things were different.

Here's the deal. Right before sixth period my friend, Tyler, told me that I was too smart. At first, I thought he said that because of the speech I gave in English class this morning that the teacher really, really liked. But the more I thought about it, the more I realized he meant something more. He wasn't saying I was smart because he was jealous or because he wanted to compliment me in that weird, backwards sort of way people sometimes use. He said "too smart" as if it was a bad thing.

So, I asked Tyler what he meant by that comment and he said that sometimes being smart is intimidating to people. When I asked him which "people" were intimidated, he said he was talking about guys. Of course, he told me he wasn't intimidated, but he said he knows a lot of guys who feel stupid around girls who know a lot and seem good at a lot of stuff. He said if I ever want a boyfriend, I have to make sure the guy feels smarter than me.

What is that all about?!?!?

I'm totally confused...why wouldn't a guy like to have a smart girlfriend? I asked Tyler if he meant I should play dumb and he said that it wasn't exactly like playing dumb, but that I would need to sound less smart so the guy would feel like he knows more. He said being smart is a good thing, but only when the guy feels smarter.

I'd hate to think Tyler is right on this. I am so frustrated! All my life, people have encouraged me to use my brain and to be excellent in all that I do. My parents have always said that my mind is a gift from God. How can my friends think so differently? OK, maybe it's not all my friends...but I trusted Tyler and in the past he's given good advice. Is he right? Do I need to appear less smart in front of my friends? God, you know that I totally want a boyfriend, but I don't think I can pretend to be something I'm not — not even for a guy.

I told my older sister about Tyler on the car ride home and she said that some guys do expect the girl to step back so they feel smarter and more powerful; but she said that isn't a good thing. She said that being a smart girl is not always easy, but that there are plenty of guys who like smart girls and will like me for who I am.

God, I don't think you would ever want me to give up a gift you've given me for the sake of another person who just wants to feel more in control. I know there's a lot of pressure to be a certain way because I really like to be liked, but my sister told me that if I live controlled by what people say—like Tyler—I'll always be frustrated. That's definitely how I feel right now, but how will I feel tomorrow?

Think about it...

＊ *Is it true that guys back off from smart girls? Why?*

＊ *How can you relate to Sara's story?*

＊ *Have you ever hidden something you do well because you didn't want to intimidate guys? Was it worth it?*

＊ *Do you think a girl should ever hide something she does well?*

A Mixed Message About Leadership

I'm a leader. I just am. I can hardly help it. I've taken spiritual gifts test, and they all come out the same: I'm a leader. When I'm with a group of people and we need to make a decision, heads usually turn in my direction. It's not like I have to lead or anything. I'm really fine with other people leading, but if there's no leader, I usually step up to the plate and do it.

I love studying leaders. I think Winston Churchill was pretty amazing. But don't get me wrong. I also like leaders on TV, especially female leaders. Oprah Winfrey rocks for the way she shares strong convictions one minute, and then cries the next. Katie Couric from "The Today Show" is a master at asking hard questions, but not being too pushy.

These women are some of my heroes. They are experts at being the kind of leader I crave, and pray, to be: a leader of gentle strength. Why do I believe "gentle strength" is so important? Well, first because that's who Jesus was. He wept with compassion and yet he overturned tables in the Temple. He mourned over the death of his friend, but he also taught with conviction and without hesitation.

Frankly, I think gentle strength is something Jesus wants for both guys and girls, but it's probably even more important for girls because of the expectations people tend to have for us. They either expect us to overemphasize being gentle and end up wimpy. Or they expect our pendulum to swing the other direction so that we overemphasize the strength part and accuse us of being _____ (word that rhymes with "witches").

The kind of girl I want to be shares her opinions when she disagrees with someone, but leaves the conversation as an even closer friend than when it started. She asks others to help her with stuff, but really cares more about them than getting a job done. And when she drops the ball, she doesn't make up excuses or blame others, but instead takes responsibility.

I know I can't be that kind of leader on my own. I need help. I'm in student government and I've asked some of the guys who are in it also to help me. They're like my radar. If I'm being too gentle, I want them to tell me. And if I'm being too strong, they need to speak up about it.

Real Guys

Ever thought of running for President of the United States? How about president of your class? Or maybe just taking the gifts and skills that God has given you to impact others?

Sometimes we can fear that the more we lead, the more guys will be scared of us. We asked our real guys if this was true.

When a girl is a leader, does it make you want to date her more, or less?

Drew W.: "When a girl is a positive leader, it makes me more interested in having a relationship with her. However, if she is over-controlling, it's a massive bummer."

Chris J.: "I know this girl who is so pushy that no guys want to be around her. Including me. But if a girl is just herself and showing that she can influence others, that makes her more attractive."

E.J. Y.: "It really has no effect on me. A pushy girl is a turn-off. But a girl who is nice to me is a turn-on. It also depends on how she treats other people around her."

Jonathan M.: "It depends on the girl. If she is too pushy, then I don't like it. But if she is really nice, then maybe."

Michael K.: "If a girl is a leader who respects others, then I would have a deeper respect for her both as a leader and as a girl. If she just pushes everyone around, then I'd lose respect for her."

Kevin C.: "Female leaders can sometimes come off too strong or snobby. But a good character and strength to stand for what she believes in are very attractive to me. But she's got to be able to admit that she's wrong at times. I appreciate gentle strength more than a forceful attitude."

So maybe this mixed message isn't so bad after all. Maybe it's all that Jesus wants us to be.

* *Do you view yourself as a leader? Why?*

* *Do you think it's true that Jesus wants male and female leaders to be examples of gentle strength? Why?*

* *When you're talking with people who aren't Christians, is it a good idea to use Jesus as an example of a leader? Why?*

* *Who's a leader that you respect? What do you like most about him or her? Is he or she an example of gentle strength? Why?*

* *You were created to influence others and God will call you to lead at times. What do you need to change in your life to become more of a leader?*

Then take a minute and ask God to help you change them.

 # The Great and Gross Period

How did you feel when you got your first period? Confused? Freaked? Psyched? Embarrassed? All the above?

Getting your period can simultaneously feel like a badge of honor and a mark of shame. Usually much more is made of the annoyance of the period and how to hide it or deodorize it, rather than celebrating the fact that it is an important indicator of a girl's transition into a young woman.

Brenda Lane Richardson and Elane Rehr have written a book that you might want to read. It's called 101 Ways to Help Your Daughter Love Her Body, so maybe your mom or step-mom might want to read it with you. When it comes to menstruation, they write:

> Rather than teach (our daughters) that menstruation is something they have to suffer through, we can reframe the notion so our girls can view it as the gift it is – though this doesn't rule out expressions of annoyance and anger. One way to reframe menstruation for your daughter is to tell her that in ancient Egypt, farmers knew that when the Nile overflowed the riverbanks and flooded the land there would be much inconvenience, but that once the waters receded, the land would be nutrient rich and supportive of tremendous growth. Tell her that the relationship between her body and her period is fairly similar – that there can be some inconvenience, but that her cycle signals the release of enriching hormones that contribute to a look of health and vitality and signal the start of physical and creative growth.

> Brenda Lane Richardson and Elane Rehr, *101 Ways to Help Your Daughter Love Her Body* (New York: Harper Collins, 2001), 148.

OK, so maybe you can't imagine cuddling up with your mom and talking about the Nile and your period, but the authors have a good point. In the midst of the cramps and yuckiness that come with that time of the month, your period is something you have a girl that guys don't have. It's what may allow you someday to get pregnant and have a baby.

Think about it...

* *How will you view your period differently from now on? Why?*

* *How might this change how you feel about yourself?*

* *If you had a daughter, what would you want to tell her about having her period?*

* *If you haven't gotten your period yet, how do you feel about that? What would you tell your future daughter if she was your age and hadn't gotten her period yet?*

Tough Questions

Read the following questions and circle your best answer. Along the way, you might want to stop and think about why you answer the way you do, and what this tells you about the way you view yourself.

1. **You finally get to talk to Ben, the guy you've had a crush on all year. You notice that he looks at your chest. And then he does it a second time. And a third. This is no accident. He's doing it on purpose. You...**

   A. Run away screaming.

   B. Stick your chest out a little further.

   C. Ask him if there's a stain on your shirt.

   D. Tell your friends about it at lunch. While you act like you're angry, you're secretly pleased.

   E. Other?

OK, now imagine instead of it being Ben, it's another guy named Trey, who others consider to be one of the biggest losers at school. Then what would you do?

2. **It's the winter formal and you're going with Jason, who is one of the coolest guys you've ever liked. You can't believe he asked you. You go shopping for a dress. Are you more likely to wear...**

   A. A sleek, form-fitting short black dress.

   B. A frilly pink dress with big poofy sleeves and a very long skirt.

   C. A killer strapless white dress.

   D. A classy blue dress with short cap sleeves with a skirt that reaches your calves.

   E. Other?

OK, imagine that instead of Jason, you're going with Micah. He's nice and everything, but you don't like him at all. Then what would you wear?

3. **History is your favorite subject. In a discussion on the World Wars, you raise your hand to answer more questions than anyone else in the room. You hear another kid snickering at you after you've answered your last question. Now the teacher asks something that you totally know. No one else is raising their hand. You...**

   A. Raise your hand anyway. Hey, you know the answer.

   B. Keep your hand down. Wouldn't want to be too know-it-all or anything.

   C. Whisper the answer to a friend who needs help with their oral participation grade.

   D. Decide not to answer, but after class, you ask a friend if you're talking too much in class.

   E. Other?

Now imagine that a guy you like is in the class. Then how would you respond?

4. In your small group discussion at your youth group, your boyfriend makes a mistake. He starts talking about how it's a proven scientific fact that evolution is wrong. You know that science can't "prove" evolution as either fact or fiction. You...

    A. Keep your mouth shut so you don't embarrass him.

    B. Tell him afterwards that that's not really true.

    C. Correct him in front of the group.

    D. Make distracting dinosaur noises during the rest of the discussion.

    E. Other?

Now imagine that it's not your boyfriend, but just an average guy at your youth group. Then what would you do?

Think about it (and maybe talk these over with a friend):

∗ Why don't we act the same way around everyone—why do we act differently around certain people?

∗ On a scale of 1-10, (10=huge problem, 1=no big deal), how big a problem is it if we act differently around different people?

∗ If you go to church, do you find that you act differently around your church friends than your school friends? Why?

∗ Do you agree that sometimes girls use their bodies to get guys' attention, and other times they get insulted when a guy they don't like stares at them? Why?

∗ Do you think it's true that sometimes girls act more or less smart if there's a guy around that they like? Explain your answer.

∗ How does all of this tie in to self-image?

Your Body: Tool or Enemy?

Put a checkmark by any statement that reflects how you feel about your body.

❑ *Sometimes I wear a short skirt to get guys' attention.*

❑ *Some days I feel so ugly that I wish I could stay home from school so that I wouldn't have to face anyone.*

❑ *I try to buy bras that make my chest look bigger.*

❑ *When I'm putting on my make-up, I often hope that it will make a guy interested in me.*

❑ *I've gone to pool parties and avoided taking off my T-shirt or walking around in my bathing suit.*

❑ *Some days I feel like I'll never be pretty. I grab my baggy jeans and sweatshirt and just go casual.*

❑ *When I choose clothes, I think more about what guys would like than what girls would like.*

❑ *When I don't like how I look, I often avoid eye contact with other people, even when I'm talking with them.*

❑ *I flip through teen magazines, hoping to pick up a hair or make-up tip that will make me more attractive to others.*

❑ *When I get my haircut, I feel better about myself and want to go hang out with guys.*

❑ *When I go with my dad for donuts on Saturday morning, if I've not showered or really even brushed my hair, I try to avoid other kids from school.*

Think about it:

∗ *Which of the statements in the above activity "Your Body: Tool or Enemy" have to do with viewing your body as a tool? Seeing your body as an enemy?*

∗ *Did you check more sentences about your body being a tool, or an enemy? Why? How do you feel about that?*

∗ *In the past, how have you used your body to get attention? Relationships? Something else you needed? How has today's chapter challenged you?*

∗ *If God was to speak to you about your thought life, and how you honor him with your body, what would he say?*

Weapon or Enemy:
A Conversation
Between Your Body and Your Body

"I've got to take what I've got and work it. Get me some male attention. Show off these legs. Wear that skirt a little bit shorter. Wear those heels a little big higher. How else are my legs going to look all muscular and tight?"

"My legs are so pudgy. My thighs are too big and my calves are too round. I can't compete. I've got to cover them up with baggy pants that make me look like I don't really care about how I look."

"Baggy pants? You've got to be kidding. If I'm going to wear pants, they're going to be tight. Curve right around my butt and show off the results of all of those leg lifts."

"The only thing worse than my legs is my stomach. It's so fat. I can pinch 2 inches of flab. I look like the Goodyear tire man. If I wear my blouse untucked, maybe I can go to the party tonight."

"Rule #1: my midriff must show. Guys like that. Something about a girl's stomach gets into a guy's head. Maybe because it's close to her chest. Good thing I bought the Miracle Bra. Makes me look bigger. Gives me more cleavage. I think those chest press exercises I've been doing have made me bigger too."

"The last thing I want is guys staring at my chest. Sure, they start at my face, but eventually, they look about eight inches south. So gross. That baggy sweater I borrowed from my dad's closet should hide me."

"Where's that strapless dress when I need it?"

"No way am I going out tonight. I'm ashamed of myself. Sometimes when I look in the mirror, I want to shrivel up and disappear."

"When I look in the mirror, I see my best asset."

"I'm hideous."

"I'm your best weapon."

"I'm your worst enemy."

Advice from a Guy

I just don't get it. Why do girls hate their bodies one minute and the next minute think their body is their main way to get attention? It's like a teeter totter. One minute up. The next minute down.

Everywhere I go, I see this problem. People think that the body is evil. So they treat it like their enemy. Or they figure, "hey if my body can get me something I want, like attention or relationships, I can use my body to get it. Primp it, paint it, flaunt it!"

Either way you slice it, neither one really leaves people feeling more special. God wants us to genuinely love how he has made us.

Paul

So do you think Paul is right? If a guy loved you so much that he offered to take a bullet for you, how would you feel?

This guy, Paul, was actually a real person. He was the Apostle Paul, whose life and letters make up more than half of the New Testament.

Way back in the first century, there were a bunch of people who believed in "Gnosticism" (pronounced nah-sti-cism). They thought that all human bodies (male and female) were evil. Influenced by the Greeks (those guys in togas), Gnostics thought God could never be part of the material world, so He could never be part of someone's body.

So people who agreed with this did one of two things:

1. They thought their bodies were bad, very bad. They shouldn't enjoy their bodies because God couldn't be in them.

2. OR they figured that if God wasn't a part of their bodies, they could do whatever they wanted to with them, which included all sorts of partying, drinking, and sex.

Although Paul's letters never mention the term "Gnosticism," we figure that since Paul was a practical guy, he wanted his ideas to relate to what people were going through. Which meant Gnosticism 2,000 years ago. And still means some of the mixed messages we girls believe now.

Your body is made to honor God

Look up 1 Corinthians. Lots of the people who lived in Corinth thought their bodies were evil. As a result, some of them partied. Others decided to ignore their bodies as much as possible. Paul had some different advice.

In 1 Corinthians 6:19-20, he writes, "Do you not know that your body is a temple of the Holy Spirit, who is in you, whom you have received from God? You are not your own; you were bought at a price. Therefore honor God with your body."

The price that's been paid for you isn't by Visa or Master Card. It's that God sent His own son, Jesus, to die on a cross for you. Both the Jews and the Romans hated the cross and considered it one of the most agonizing ways to die. Since nails were pounded into Jesus' hands and feet on the cross, honor God with our body—it's the least we can do.

Real Girls

OK, hopefully by now you understand what we mean by mixed messages. But how does this relate to the real life of a teenage girl? We asked our real girls:

What mixed messages can you relate to, and what truth would you like to send out to every girl around the world to correct the mixup?

Erica M.: "It's confusing that we're supposed to be ourselves, but not supposed to be too different. I think the truth is that we should be ourselves, period."

Elaine W.: "I can relate to the message that girls are supposed to be pretty, but not try too hard to look pretty. I wish girls could just walk around being themselves, without worrying what others will think."

Searcy. C.: "I can relate to lots of them. Be strong, but not intimidating. Be sexy, but don't be a slut. Wear make-up, but look natural. I think the truth is that girls should just be themselves. It's too hard dealing with all those messages. Just act the way you want to act. And if you give your life to the Lord, it will be forever easier."

Christy G.: "Be athletic and strong, but still be feminine. Be sexy, but not a slut. The truth is that girls should just be themselves. If you're being fake, guys don't even see the real you. They're looking at a fake person."

Macall R.: "I feel like I am supposed to be a strong person who can handle everything. Yet at the same time, I'm supposed to be completely helpless and let guys do everything for me. I wish girls would see that that they can and should do things for themselves, but they don't have to have it all together."

Brittany H.: "Be strong, but not too strong. Since I go to an all girls school, they emphasize being confident in ourselves. So when I'm with guys, I open doors for myself, handle problems by myself and am pretty self-sufficient. That's intimidating to guys, I guess. And I can also relate to the message of be smart, but not too smart. I always find myself dumbing down around guys so I don't scare them away. I'm still wrestling with all this, but I wish we girls were just comfortable with who we are."

Emily C.: "Be skinny, but not too skinny. Society pushes girls to be thin but then points its finger at girls who have eating disorders or are too thin. Playing the skinny game can be so destructive. I wish girls knew how to love their bodies."

Right...
and this applies to my life...how?

Which of the mixed message below can you most relate to? Least relate to? Why?

Be sexy, but not a slut.
Be smart, but not too smart.
Be strong, but not too strong.
Other _____

Your body is a place where God dwells

If you've decided to follow Jesus and given your life to him, by his Holy Spirit, God lives inside you. Your body isn't evil. It's not your enemy. Nor is it something whose main purpose is to get guys' attention. It's God's house. It's where he lives.

Every part of you is part of that temple. Your eyes are like the stained-glass windows that let God's light shine out. Your voice is like the musical instruments that share about him. Your arms welcome and serve others who are looking for help.

Think about it...

* *Think about that body part that you don't like. Just one. How does it make you feel to realize you were handcrafted by God? That he loves you as you are? How does this challenge you?*

* *God is present with you as you make decisions of how to use your body. What do you think God's perspective is about people using their body to get the attention of others? For sinful purposes?*

* *How can God change your perspective about your body? About using your body only to honor God?*

mirror mirror

Kara Powell and Kendall Payne

Preoccupation
with body and appearance

❋ **THE SCULPTOR**
No Ordinary Work of Art

❋ **BODY QUIZ**
The Numbers Don't Lie

❋ **TO LIKE OR NOT TO LIKE**
Easier Said Than Done

❋ Plus: Cutting: The Dirty Secrets About the Troubling Act

* Worry Warts

In high school, I had a love/hate relationship with my bathroom mirror. On the one hand, it was the only way to find out how I looked. On the other hand, I often frowned at what I saw.

I especially hated it on those days when zits blanketed my face. And that was pretty much every day, which meant my mirror and I weren't the best of friends.

On the days I had more acne, I'd avoid looking people in the eye. I'd still talk with them, but I'd look at the ground. At their shoulder. At the person skateboarding behind them. Anywhere but at their face. I figured that if I didn't look at their face, they wouldn't look at my face, and then I'd be OK.

Or if I had acne on my right cheek, I'd stand facing to the right so that everyone would see my left cheek more than my right cheek. I worked hard at it, and got pretty good at facing left, right, north, or south. Whatever was needed to shield the pimply part of me.

Sometimes I'd forget about the Mount St. Helens pimple erupting just to the right of my nose. I'd be so into the conversation that I'd forget there was something I had to camouflage. But that never lasted long. And when I remembered, I'd resume my hide-my-face tactics.

20% of women say they are completely satisfied with their bodies. (Survey for People magazine in the article "How Do I Look?," _People_ magazine, September 4, 2000, 114.) Given the women and girls you know, would you say that number is too high, too low, or just right?

I tried every make-up trick in the book. From flesh covered lotion to green minimizing cream to dabbing Visine onto my zits to get the red out. None of it made them disappear, and usually it made them even worse.

The funny (or maybe not-so-funny) thing is that zits didn't just change how I felt about how I looked. They changed how I felt about me. They poisoned how I felt about hanging out with friends. They contaminated how I felt about talking to the guy I liked. Those few red bumps changed everything about me.

I was preoccupied with them. They defined me. They described me. They made me smaller inside. They stole from me.

And the more I worried, the worse it got. No one ever likes zits, but I wish that I had been able to see them, shrug them off, and move on. Quite honestly, I wish I was able to do that today.

But instead, we females keep scorecards. My legs aren't too bad, so I get two points for those, but my hair is totally frizzy, so I lose one point. Three thousand dollars to the orthodontist who straightened out my smile, but I lose half a point because my nose is still crooked. My shoulders look good, so that's a plus, but I have too many freckles, so that's a minus

What if we could throw away the scorecard? What if we weren't so worried about counting points, but instead knew that we were perfect 10's? That despite what we disliked about our bodies, we didn't need to worry about them.

Sound like a fairy tale? Maybe. Or maybe it's just how it was supposed to be in the first place. Keep reading. No promises that you'll live "happily ever after," but you just may be able to smile at what greets you in the mirror.

A Friend, Some Ducks, and a Lesson I'll Never Forget

By Kendall

We'd been friends now for seven years. She is 5'2." Long beautiful blond hair, that comes down to her mid-back. I am 5'10". With short spunky red hair. We have great times together. We can make each other laugh harder than probably anyone else. She is one of my best friends.

We are beyond the early stages of friendship where we need to impress each other. She and I have traveled many miles with each other and like a trusty old car we're still running.

One day we decided to take a walk. She had moved into a new house and we wanted to explore the neighborhood. It was a hot day and so I arrived dressed in my spandex shorts, (which is no sight to see) and loose cotton tee-shirt. She wore something similar.

As we started our trek we began the conversation with the normal downloads of our lives: love lives, struggles, greatest pleasures and how many and how large are the zits on our faces..."I mean really, don't tell me you didn't see it! After all if your friends can't tell you the truth, who will?"

We have some deep discussion about the influence of our lives and what we could be doing versus what we actually are doing. And we vow to start making more of a difference and for a second we feel better. We see a garage sale and rummage through someone else's trash trying to find a treasure of our own. But we have no such luck. We kept walking.

The terrain was hilly. I was sweating considerably and grateful that my friend was at my side and not some guy I was trying to impress. Because of my fair skin, when I get hot my face turns the color of a ripe red tomato, it's not a pretty sight! We looked at all the houses and commented on what we liked, loved and what we'd be to drive home to at night. And within about a half an hour we found ourselves at a picturesque lake. Being exhausted from the heat and being that we like to liberally spice our "workouts" with large moments of relaxation we soon found ourselves on a patch of grass, in the shade, reclining.

Before long, a small family of three came walking along the sidewalk. A daddy, a mommy and their little boy who had a plastic bag with old bread pieces in it. He was hurling them over the metal pole that separated the concrete pavement from the murky lake water. The boy would scream with delight when the ducks would rush the soggy mass and swim away. We sat in complete enjoyment of such a simple act bringing so much pleasure to this little boy. His parents gave us apologetic smiles, but we just smiled back. No bother. After ten minutes or so he ran out of ammunition, became distracted and the family moved. We were alone again.

It started pretty simple. We began to amuse ourselves by naming the ducks. One was following another and so we assumed they were boyfriend and girlfriend. We started making up voices for them. Each one became a new and interesting character. I think for a second we remembered what it was like to be 5 years old again. Just like that little boy.

We decided that one duck was royalty, disguised as a peasant, hiding out in this part of the lake (she was the one who became more and more beautiful the more you looked at her). One was a world traveler and had many stories to tell (he was the old one). One was the bully that tried to steal another's girlfriend (he was the biggest duck chasing the first two ducks we saw). So wrapped up in the story we had written for these ducks, I was caught off guard by another that came swimming into the scene. It was a swan.

Continued on next page...

Where the others were speckled, this one was without spot. While the others were little, cute and plain, this one was long, beautiful and dramatic. And when the others would swim, it was with small strokes this one seemed to glide across the lake without effort. It was so different.

I said, "That swan is the most beautiful of them all." It seemed obvious to me that no other duck could even compete with this swan. But to my surprise, my friend said, "No. I don't agree. I liked the little ducks better." I couldn't believe it!

I started to think about all these animals that we had now made into friends, by naming them and imagining their life stories. I wondered what the little mallards thought of the swan.

I wondered, if they had the opportunity, would the little mallards go to a "duck salon" and bleach all their feathers white? Would they do exercises to try to lengthen their necks? Would they take lessons on gliding and gracefulness? Would they visit the plastic surgeon and get beak jobs? And I realized that those were some of the stupidest thoughts I'd ever had.

Ducks don't think that way. They are happy with themselves. God made them a certain way and they don't spend their time wishing they were something different, preoccupied with desires to be someone else.

From this simple, stupid thought, it suddenly hit me. How many times have I watched "Friends" and wished I could fit into Jennifer Aniston's jeans? How many times have I thought, "If I just workout every day I could look like Gwyneth Paltrow"? Or wanted to have Winona Ryders big brown eyes...when mine are blue.

Why do I do this to myself? Why do I always want to be something I'm not? Why aren't I happy with the way God chose to make me?" And I thought about the ducks again. What a tragedy and foolish pursuit it would be if even one tried to be something it's obviously not. And again I felt stupid, but this time not for thinking about the ducks.

Scarface

I finally got it.

Guess where? In my college psychology class, of all places. For days our professor had been going on and on about different experiments. I listened and took notes, not so much because I cared, but because I wanted to pass the class.

Then I got it.

In between hearing about dogs salivating, children playing with dolls, and television violence, the prof talked about an experiment that I'll call "The Scarface Project."

Some researchers called a bunch of people into their offices and explained, "We want to see how strangers respond to you when you have a scar on your face. So we're going to take each of you into a separate room and use make-up to put a big, red scar on your left cheek."

So every person went into their own small room. There were only five things in each room: the make-up, the person doing the make-up, the person getting the scar, and two chairs for them both to sit on. Notice anything missing? Think hard. Got it yet? How about a mirror?

The people getting the scars on their faces couldn't see what was happening to them. Once the make-up person was done, they held up mirrors so that folks could see their scars. Then each make-up person took back the mirror and said, "Now I'm going to put a little finishing powder on your scar just so it doesn't smear."

But here's the trick: instead of putting finishing powder on their scars, the make-up people actually used a tissue to remove the scar. So now people thought they had a scar, but they had no scar.

The Scar-less people went out into the lobbies of doctors' offices, hotels, and airports. Overwhelmingly, the Scar-less folks came back and reported that people were rude and less kind to them. Plus they said people stared at their scar!

Think about it. The Scar-less people thought something was wrong with them physically, and that everyone else noticed it and acted differently. In reality, it was all in their imagination.

That's kind of like thinking everybody notices your bad hair day, or your zits, or the bar-b-q sauce stain on your shirt. Frankly, everyone else is so worried about their own bad hair, zits, and stains that they don't have time or energy to notice yours.

Think about it...

* When was the last time you didn't like how you looked? Why?
* At the time, did you feel like people noticed that part of your body more?
* How did it make you feel about yourself? Why?
* Is it true that "everybody else is so worried about their own bad hair, zits, and stains that they don't have time or energy to notice yours." Why?

    Psychologists have identified a phenomenon that teenagers experience called the "imaginary audience." It's that feeling that comes over you at times when you feel all eyes are on you. Any blunder you make, any physical imperfection you have is not only noticed, but magnified, in the eyes of the world around you.

* When have you experienced this feeling like you just know people are staring at that zit on your face? Describe the feeling.
* The next time that you don't like your hair, or shirt, or lipstick, what do you want to keep in mind?

Breasts

*It's rare to find a girl who doesn't worry about her breasts.
Circle any of the statements that you can relate to.*

* *I got my first bra way later than most of my friends.*

* *I can't even ask my brother to pass a chicken breast without getting embarrassed.*

* *Guys never stare at my chest.*

* *I'm embarrassed to walk through the bra section of a department store.*

* *I notice guys staring at my chest.*

* *One of my breasts is bigger than the other.*

* *I have let a guy touch my breasts.*

* *My chest is so big that it's causing me back pain.*

* *My breasts got really big really fast.*

* *I buy bras with lots of padding – Wonder Bras, Miracle Bras – bring 'em on.*

* *I don't like shopping for bras.*

* *I can't imagine ever letting a guy touch my breasts.*

* *I still don't wear a bra.*

* *When I take off my clothes to take a shower, I avoid looking at my breasts in the mirror.*

* *I love shopping for bras.*

Think about it...

* *Which of these statements did you relate to the most? Why? How do you feel about that?*
* *Why do you think such a big deal is made about breasts?*
* *If there were no guys on the planet, would breasts be such a big deal? Why?*

It turns out that breast size could make a difference in how we feel about ourselves. In a study of 54 girls, the bigger the breast size, the better the self-image. The girls in this study were 10-14 year-olds.[1]

Do you think that girls your age are more or less likely to base their self-image on their breast size? Why?

[1] Gail B. Slap, et al. "Evolving Self-Image, Pubertal Manifestations, and Pubertal Hormones: Preliminary Findings in Young Adolescent Girls", Journal of Adolescent Health, 1994: Volume 15, 327-335.

I Wish I Could Be a Guy

Sometimes I wish I could be a guy.

Sure, I know that some of them stress about how they look. They're not tall enough, or buff enough, or thin enough, or handsome enough.

But it's not as bad as when you're a girl. Guys are in a battle. We girls are in a war.

See, when guys go through puberty, they gain weight. They get more muscles. But our culture tells guys that gaining weight and getting more muscles is good.

Girls also gain weight and hips. But here's the difference: our culture screams to girls that gaining weight and hips is bad. Small is good. Big is bad.

Let me be more clear.

Puberty Changes + Guys = Good
Puberty Changes + Girls = Bad

No wonder I worry so much.
I'm fighting my biology.

Did You Know....

According to the Harvard Project on Women's Psychology and Girls' Development, many girls think well of themselves in elementary school but by the time they turn 12, their self-confidence and acceptance of their body image plummets.

P. Orenstein, *Schoolgirls*: Young Women, Self-Esteem, and the Confidence Gap (New York: Doubleday, 1994).

Why I Cut Myself

by Andrea

I will never really know what made me actually pick up the knife and do it the first time. That day began like any other. I went to school for my zero hour Jazz band class and then went off to my other classes. Sean, my boyfriend at the time, made some wisecrack at lunch about how he thought that I was cheating on him. A few hours later, I fell asleep in a practice room during my last class and woke up to Sean telling me that school was out for the day and he was ready to take me home. I soon noticed that while I was asleep, I had gnawed one of my knuckles to the point of nearly bleeding and had not realized it.

A few hours later, as I was getting ready to go play for graduation, I sat in my bathroom and noticed my pocket knife on the counter. I had the sudden impulse to open it up and do something. I sat down, opened it up and cut a small slit in the skin at the top of my leg, where it wouldn't be seen. It didn't really hurt, so I didn't think anything of it. Then I found myself cutting on my arm, twice. Pulling the knife over my skin until it not only broke, but bled since my knife was new and sharp, sent a funny feeling down my spine and into the pit of my stomach. When I took my shower, it hurt even more.

What made me do it? I still don't know. It felt like I had taken a great weight off my shoulders. Or at least I could ignore it for a little while longer.

But I should go back a few years to junior high, when I returned to the world of public school after being home schooled. I've never really had a good self-image. Because I grew up in a conservative Christian home, I could not wear what most of what the other girls did, especially in junior high and high school.

My hair was not the same, and I was fully developed and had a large chest years before the other girls. Many people I thought of as friends teased me and made me feel unattractive and unimportant.

There were so many other little things, though, that made me depressed to begin with. Yearning to fit in socially led me into dating. And with dating came jealous friends who convinced me that I was a terrible friend who was worthless and couldn't do anything right, ever. Also, because I tend to be a friendly, sometimes flirty person, boyfriends tried to clamp down and make me change my personality completely to be more complacent. By my junior year of high school, I hated myself. I was ugly and worthless in my eyes.

Nine months after Sean and I started dating, I found cutting to be my "salvation." When I cut, I could justify that I was horrible; punishing myself for all the things I was convinced that I did wrong. I felt a little guilty, because somewhere in the back of my mind I could remember a verse from the Bible saying that we were God's temple, so technically it was the wrong thing to be doing. But it felt so good that I ignored the guilt. It never lasted long anyway.

Let me give you a small analogy. I felt like inside of me there was a glass. Since I did not know how to deal with my pain, it would pour into my glass a little at a time. After a while, the glass would get so full that it would spill over a little and then I would cry at random, for no real reason. The glass would empty a little when I did, and I could go on as if nothing had happened.

As I began to notice my depression, I found that the cup was spilling over more often. It went from once a month, to once a week, to several times a week that I would close myself in my room and cry. When I began to cut, I felt that the glass would do better than just slightly empty. It dumped out lots of water.

Five to six weeks after I began cutting, I found myself addicted to it. There would be periods of time, some as
Continued on next page....

short as a few minutes and some as long as an hour or more, where I had the sudden urge to cut myself. It didn't matter how or with what, but I needed to do it. Like any addiction, I needed it no matter how or what it costed. I did not have any idea of how I was going to stop, and no real desire to other than that I knew it was wrong to feel the way I did.

I came home from counseling at a Christian camp and knew I had to tell someone what was going on. I couldn't tell my mom. Whenever I was sad, my mom had always been the one to tell me that "It must be that time of the month again. You have a loving, supportive family, and everyone else has it off worse than you do. You have no reason to be depressed. Give it a few days and you'll be over it."

No one at my church would have understood. So many people at church always told my mom "your daughter is always happy, nothing keeps her down. She can handle anything!" They had no idea.

Think about it...

* Given Andrea's story, how do you think cutting relates to how people feel about themselves? Explain.

* Have you ever felt like you wanted to cut yourself? Why?

* What did, or do, you do about that feeling?

* What helped Andrea get out of her addiction?

* How does that relate to you?

  Maybe it's not cutting, but are you addicted to other things or do certain things because you feel bad about yourself? (Like eating, or shopping, or exercising, or computer.) Explain.

* What hope and help can you draw from Andrea's story?

Telling my dad was the hardest thing I've ever done. To show my dad that his little girl had such a problem, and to cause him the pain that I saw in his eyes was hard. But I did it. My parents took me to the doctor, who put me on medication and referred us to a therapist, and that was where I spent most of my summer before we moved.

It is amazing how the person who looks the happiest can be the most miserable. The façade can get so perfect that even the people who love you the most are blind to it. I wish I could say that having my parents send me to therapy helped me stop. I wish I could tell you that, but it would be a lie. It was not until the middle of my senior year of high school that the urges went away.

Due to a job change, my family moved from Washington to California. Senior year is a hard time to leave your friends and make new ones, but remember I'm always a friendly person.

It was in California that I met Kym and Daniel. I found that I wasn't alone, and someone other than my parents who cared that I had a problem (parents have to care). Kym was a cutter too, but no one knew it. Her façade was like mine, and she hadn't broken yet. We became best friends, and after talking and hanging out together, I found that, for a time, my cutting subsided a little.

In January I met Daniel. I stole his seat in English class, and that started one of the best friendships I've ever had. There were times when Daniel and I would spend entire afternoons talking about everything. He was the one person who made me talk through how I felt when the knife went into my skin. I soon stopped cutting altogether. Why did I stop? I think it was because I knew there was someone my age who loved me, and who would do anything to help me stop.

It has taken some time to heal to the point that I can believe in myself again. I can usually look in the mirror and see someone pleasant, that people love to be around, instead of a monster. I say "usually" because it will take even more time before the healing process will be finished. Sometimes I still have a hard time believing that my life matters, and at those times the urges come again. But what I do know is that I have family and friends who will be there whenever I need help. People who love me enough to hold me when I fall.

The Sculptor

In front of me sits a brick of clay. Not just any old clay. The best clay available anywhere. It cost me a lot, but it's worth it.

I know exactly what I want to sculpt. I've got this mental picture of a beautiful girl. She's vibrant. She's perfect. She's her.

I start by shaping her body. I've given a lot of thought to how I want her to look. What curves I want where. How long I want her legs. How her arms should hang. The shape of her hips and breasts. I have planned every single square inch of her.

Next I move to her face. I'm extra careful here. With every touch of my hand, every swipe of my palm, I create a face that takes my breath away. Her eyes are deep, glowing, magnetic. Her nose is amazing. Her mouth is unlike all others.

Now onto her hair. I won't stop until I get it just right. Just the right texture, body, and color. She'll probably complain, but the truth is that I've never created any better than her.

She's my masterpiece.

OK, you might have guessed it by now, but this is no ordinary sculptor. He's the most well-known sculptor in all of history. And many think he does the best work. his name? God.

And you are his project, his masterpiece. He has NEVER created anyone who is more beautiful than you. He's the perfect artist, and you are his result.

Unlike every other artist, He never makes a mistake. He never has to start over. He had in mind what you were going to look like when he created you in your mom's womb, and you've come out just right.

The author of Psalm 139 realized this, and wanted to let God know how he felt about God's artwork. He wrote,

Oh yes, you shaped me first inside, then out;
You formed me in my mother's womb.
I thank you, High God – you're breathtaking!
Body and soul, I am marvelously made!
I worship in adoration – what a creation!
You know me inside and out,
You know every bone in my body;
You know exactly how I was made, bit by bit,
How I was sculpted from nothing into something.

Psalm 139:13-15, The Message.

Think about it:

* In an average day, how much time do you spend thinking about how you look?
* Should you spend more or less time thinking about how you look? Why?
* Which of the above lines from Psalm 139 stands out to you? Why?
* Let's say that line was stamped on every mirror you could look into.
  How would that change how you felt when you looked in the mirror?

Body Quiz

Let's pretend the picture below is you.

Put a star next to every part of your body that you like.
Circle every part of your body that you don't like.

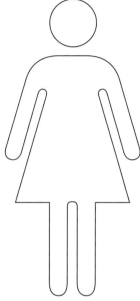

Write the number of stars you have here _____

Write the number of circles you have here _____

Subtract the circles from the stars.
So if you had 7 stars and 5 circles, you would end up with 2.
If you had 5 stars and 8 circles, you would end up with -3....

If you ended up with:

A positive number (0, 1, 2, 3, 4, 5, 6, etc.):
Congratulations. You like more about your body than you dislike. And that's pretty rare. If your score was really high, beware of being too cocky. If your score was really low, those circles might soon catch up to those stars and change your score. Either way, choose 3 circles above and write what you think God would say to you about that body part.

A negative number (-1, -2, -3, -4, -5, -6, etc.):
You're probably not feeling too good about your body these days. It's way easier for you to think about things you don't like about your body than what you do like. Let's try to change that a bit. Choose 3 circles above and write what you think God would say to you about that body part.

Hey! Did you notice...
That no matter what your score was, we asked you to choose 3 circles and write down what God would say about that body part. No matter how you feel about your body right this second, whether you love it or despise it, it's always a good idea to remember what God would say. You're just the finished product. But he's the artist.

✳ To Like or Not To Like

Do this: As you read each statement below, make an "x" on the continuum to indicate your response.

I like my hair.
Totally false___ Kinda false____ Middle___ Kinda true___ Totally true

I like my nose.
Totally false___ Kinda false____ Middle___ Kinda true___ Totally true

I like my eyes.
Totally false___ Kinda false____ Middle___ Kinda true___ Totally true

I like my nose.
Totally false___ Kinda false____ Middle___ Kinda true___ Totally true

I like my mouth.
Totally false___ Kinda false____ Middle___ Kinda true___ Totally true

I like my legs.
Totally false___ Kinda false____ Middle___ Kinda true___ Totally true

I like my body.
Totally false___ Kinda false____ Middle___ Kinda true___ Totally true

I like my breasts.
Totally false___ Kinda false____ Middle___ Kinda true___ Totally true

It's easier for me to think of what I don't like about how I look than what I like.
Totally false___ Kinda false____ Middle___ Kinda true___ Totally true

Kids at school look at me and notice the things I don't like about myself.
Totally false___ Kinda false____ Middle___ Kinda true___ Totally true

My mom and/or dad say nice things about how I look.
Totally false___ Kinda false____ Middle___ Kinda true___ Totally true

My step-mom and/or step-dad say nice things about how I look.
Totally false___ Kinda false____ Middle___ Kinda true___ Totally true

I believe the nice things my parent(s)/step-parent(s) say about how I look.
Totally false___ Kinda false____ Middle___ Kinda true___ Totally true

I can think of 3 things I'd change about how I look right now.
Totally false___ Kinda false____ Middle___ Kinda true___ Totally true

I can think of 7 things I'd change about how I look right now.
Totally false___ Kinda false____ Middle___ Kinda true___ Totally true

*Everywhere I Go

**Read the following poem and then answer the
questions below it:**

Everywhere I go
People notice me.
They look at me.
They see what I hate
About me.

I'm short and squatty.
My thighs are wide.
My hair is all curly.
And my nose is huge.

On the outside
They smile at me.
But on the inside.
They think I'm ugly.
Because I am.

My mom says
I'm cute.
My step-dad says
I'm beautiful.
I say
They're wrong.

Write your responses to each of the statements below:

Yes/No *This poem describes what I feel about myself. Explain.*

Yes/No *If my close friend, _____ (name), had written this poem, I'd know what to say to
her to encourage her.*

* *Here's what I would say to my close friend after reading her poem:*

* *Of the advice I would give my good friend, which of it should I remember most to be encouraged?*

* *If I remembered this advice, my life would be better because:*

*Real Girls

Top Tips for the "Feel Like Less Than a 10" Days

We hope that you don't just read Mirror, Mirror, by yourself, but that you talk it over with your friends. But just in case, we want you to meet some real girls who will help you figure out what all this means.

They're regular girls with familiar struggles. They're dealing with the same things you are, from getting a date to the next dance to figuring out what to do after they graduate.

There's Brittany H., an 18-year-old senior who's into surfing and cooking. (Quite a combo, eh?)

Kathy W. is a 16-year-old who does flips for fun. On her cheer squad, that is.

Elaine W. is a 14-year-old who's into dancing, volleyball, chocolate, and the Lord (not in that order).

Emily C. is a junior who's into singing. Do Re Me Fa So, and all that that.

Nicole R. is a 16-year-old who plays water polo at her school. When she's not all wet, she likes clothes and make-up.

Macall R. is a senior who loves all sorts of singing. From show choir to voice lessons to regular ol' choir, Macall loves to belt it out.

Searcy C. is a freshman who loves the phone and her friends. Can anyone say "call waiting"?

Emily B. is a senior who digs tennis, art, and music. (But probably not all at once.)

Sophomore *Erica M.* is way into volleyball and photography. When she talks, she gets right to the main point.

Christy G. loves two things: being a softball pitcher, and pizza. Sounds like a pretty good Saturday afternoon.

Since we've been talking about being a perfect 10, we asked our real girls for their list of things to do to help you when you feel like less than a perfect 10. You might want to try one of these ideas the next time you're feeling more like a 6 or 7:

Kathy W.: "I put on more make-up, and I practice cheerleading because that's something I'm good at."

Nicole R.: "I wear a little more make-up and wear some cute clothes."

Emily B.: "I try to fix my hair differently, and I wear make-up."

Searcy C.: "I usually turn up my music really loud and just hang out with myself. Or I get into a hot bubble bath and give myself a home facial."

Brittany H.: "I spend some time alone and take a bath. Or I think about the good qualities that I have."

Elaine W.: "I take some time to be by myself and relax, or I dance, or play volleyball."

Christy G.: "I like to curl my hair and wear make-up. Like at Homecoming when I was dressed up and got my hair, nails and make-up done. I felt totally beautiful."

Emily C.: "I like to go shopping and get new clothes."

Macall R.: "I buy clothes I like or I practice singing."

Erica M.: "I stare at myself in the mirror until I see beauty and love the way I look."

Did You Know...

The October 2002 edition of YM reports the results of 1000 girls, 13 to 19 years-old, who were asked about their biggest beauty problems. Girls were most stressed out about their appearance in the following areas: body (44%), skin (25%), hair (9%), and facial features (9%). Only 8% said, "I'm happy the way I am."

YM, October 2002, pages 52-56.

By the age of 14, girls in the United States have become aware that their ability to succeed, if not survive, in the social order is mostly based on how they look.

Mary Ruth Laycock and Becky Dornheim, *Fat Talk*, Bloomington, 2000.

mirror mirror

by Kara Powell and Kendall

t·he WORLD

*ON CAMPUS JESUS
Are You Nervous or Excited?

*YOUR BIRTHDAY
ALL YEAR LONG
Don't Save the Wrapping Paper

*SCHOOL DAZE
Easier Said Than Done

*FOLLOW MY LEAD
You're Not Travelling Alone

*On Campus Jesus

Imagine Jesus showed up at your school campus for lunch. Where would he sit? Who would he talk to? What would he eat? What would he say?

Now imagine him hanging out with your friends. Where would they all go? What would he talk about? What would they think of him?

Get this: Jesus is on your campus. he is with your friends. Why?

Because he is present in and with you.

Yup, the moment you ask Jesus to take over your life, and to be your Savior and Lord, he comes and lives inside of you. When you show up to P.E. class, Jesus is with you. When you grab coffee after school, he's along for the ride.

How does that make you feel? Guilty? Nervous? Scared?

How about EXCITED?

How about AMAZED at the fact that as he changes you, you change the world around you.

Change the world. That's a pretty big goal. Lots of times, you might feel like you can't change anyone around you. Especially if you're struggling with self-image. You feel like you have nothing to offer. Quite honestly, you don't. You are a sinful, struggling teenager standing in a sinful, struggling world.

But as you let him change you. As you get filled with him, you end up with something to offer. It's kind of like a fountain. As you're overflowing with him, he'll splash out of you and get others wet.

Or sometimes you feel like you're too young. You think that changing the world is what people do when they're older. The truth is that you do not have to wait until you're 18, or 21, or 30 to spill Jesus onto others. You can do it right now.

Jesus himself was once a teenager, and when he was twelve, He was already teaching adults (see Luke 2:41-52). Now granted, you're not God's son or anything, but you have a relationship with God's son that gives you lots of ideas on what to say and be like.

We'd be lying to you if we didn't warn you: changing the world will cost you. It might cost you the approval of others, money, free time, or other goals. It cost Jesus his life. But quite honestly, a life that doesn't influence or impact others, that doesn't change other's lives for the better—that's a far cry from the best life God has for each of us.

Here's a really big point. If we could tattoo this point into your brain, we would. Trust us:

"You don't try to change others in order to make God like or love you more. You change others because of how much God loves you to start with."

It's a bit like a marriage. I don't surprise my husband with a new sweatshirt so that he'll love me more. I give it because of the kind of love relationship we already have.

That's how God is. He doesn't want us to earn anything from him. He wants us to obey and serve him because of the love relationship we already have with him. He simply wants our lives to be one big thank you note back to him for all he's done for us. So make your life the most creative, colorful, and breathtaking thank you card possible.

Pop Culture vs. God Culture

By Kendall

All right, it's time to admit that I have a secret of my own. I cannot watch the Victoria's Secret commercials! I find them spiritually disturbing. I have to look away.

Most guys that I hang out with are trying to honor God with their lives, their eyes and their minds. I feel bad for them when the commercial comes on TV. But I'm starting to feel just as bad for myself.

In the mall I have memorized where the store is and avoid that section at all costs. It is not the lingerie or the bras or the underwear that bother me, I happen to like all their products. It's the advertisements.

I can go from feeling fantastic all morning, self confident and sure of God's calling on my life. Then, like a bat out of hell, it comes flying at me. I catch 35 seconds of a V.S. commercial and Bam! The obsession begins.

I pass by a mirror and casually glance at my reflection when the thought hits me immediately, "Wow! I think I've gained weight. These pants don't look as good as they did 10 minutes ago. Can it happen that fast?" Absolutely nothing has changed. There is no possible way they could look any different, but somehow they do! I ask my sister, "Do you think they make my butt look big?" Her eyes roll back in her head and for the next five hours, literally, I've got "butt-on-the-brain!

I would be embarrassed and ashamed to admit all this if I wasn't positive that other women feel the exact same way. Is it normal? Is it something I will grow out of when I finally discover the meaning of life? I don't know. I sure hope so.

Nude on the Wall

The other thing that I don't understand is a clothing store that runs an ad campaign with all nude models! I was in a changing room and looked up at the poster on the wall. It was a waist-up shot of a girl cupping her breasts in her hands, staring seductively into the camera. I almost ripped it off the wall. I wanted to march myself up to the manager and say, "Do you sell clothes here or nakedness? Because I would like to buy her boobs."

I Don't Care Who You Are...Really, I Don't

The next piece of the puzzle came when I was standing in line at a Mexican fast food restaurant, ready to order my grilled chicken salad, secretly wanting a burrito. The song starts slowly wafting into my brain like the smell of fried tortilla chips to my nose. Without even realizing it, "I don't care who you are," I sing quietly to myself. "Where you're from," My toe is tapping. "Don't care what you did," my head is nodding back and forth. "As long as you" I am in full voice by this point with my eyes closed, "love me baby..." Snapping back to reality I quickly look around to see if anyone noticed my incredibly embarrassing moment. Luckily, and with very little surprise, not a single eye was on me. I still felt like a nerd!

You see, as a professional musician I have worked very hard to become a member of an elite group. We are, what my mom calls, "music snobs." This is how you become a music snob—everything that is massively popular and that everyone likes—you have to dislike. Everything that is simple—you have to say is too simple. Everything that is on the radio is—in your opinion, selling out. (But that's only because your music is not on the radio yet. When that happens, this rule will change.)

But, let me warn you, if you succeed in becoming a full-fledged music snob, never, ever, ever be caught dead singing along to a Backstreet Boys song in some cheesy little Mexican restaurant! You'll deserve to be kicked out.

Luckily no spies were there. But it got me thinking, as pop music rarely does. What are they talking about?

"I don't care who you are." Isn't that what love is all about? Caring about who your significant other is?

"Where you're from" Does that mean like another country? What if you didn't speak the same language? That would matter enough to care?

"Don't care what you did." That cracks me up! What if they're a murderer, or an insane, jealous stalker? Would you care then?

"As long as you love me baby." Oh, now it all makes sense! (Can you see the sarcasm in my type font?) So they're telling me as long as she loves him then nothing about her matters right?

Or how about these words, "I'll never break your heart, I'll
Continued on next page...

never make you cry." It's a lie! There is no humanly way that is possible!

All right, enough ranting and raving. Honestly, I don't have a problem with Backstreet Boys or any other pop music for that matter, and it is rather fun to blast it from you car stereo on late night drives when no one can make fun of you. And I don't have a problem with Victoria's Secret braziers or pink pok-a-dot pajamas. And the naked advertising ploy never once squeezed a penny out of me, but I still shop there because the clothes are cute. I only bring it up because it begs a deeper question, and uncovers a longing in the female psyche that must be looked at. Lucky for you, I'm willing to look at it. Unfortunately I'm gonna drag you along for the ride.

In Search of the Gorgeous Guy

So you like to feel beautiful, eh? And you like to feel desired by the opposite sex; that's normal! And experimenting with makeup and clothes are some healthy ways of discovering yourself. But beauty is not just skin deep. It takes a long time to learn that lesson but it's true. If you believe nothing else we say, believe that.

But what is the point of beauty, superficial or unseen, if it is not to attract? That is the goal, isn't it? To find the cutest or smartest or funniest (or whatever floats your boat) guy and get him to like you back right? Right.

So once you have zeroed in on him (or his kind) then you must set a standard. This can be any number of things; it's good to prioritize, what small "ism's" you would be willing to overlook if the major qualifications are met. Some people make lists. These can contain random information like:

1. He must love to tap dance or

2. He must have a fond affection for the game Scrabble. (These are very strange and I would not suggest making them high on your list.)

Most girls want either brown or blue or green eyes, tall or short, scrawny or ripped and so on. None of these things are bad, but you need to set a standard for more than just the physical aspects of a man. The spiritual standard, emotional standard and intellectual standard are (in the long run) far more important.

If you want the kind of guy who only cares about looks, you will have to be the kind of girl who: is always wearing the latest fashion; constantly at the gym; who spends tons of money on hair cuts, eye shadows, lip gloss and the like. Because that kind of guy is only attracted to that kind of girl.

But if you want the kind of guy who cares about God and the deeper things in life, then you need to be the kind of girl who: has big dreams for herself; who has a thriving relationship with God; who doesn't give into peer pressure easily; who has a mind of her own. Because this kind of guy is only attracted to this kind of girl.

So what are you doing to develop the character that will interest the kind of guy you want? Studying hard at school? Practicing an instrument? Volunteering at an old folks' home? Reading a fascinating book? Learning a new language? Establishing a quiet time with God? Heading out on a missions trip? Or are you plucking your eyebrows, whitening your teeth and avoiding ice cream? Someone once asked me, "How do you get self-esteem?" "That's simple," I said. "The good old fashion way… you earn it."

Your Birthday All Year Long

The best birthday gift I ever got was a phone. This was no ordinary phone, but a 900 megahertz headset phone. I love talking to people, and since the phone is one of the best ways to chat, I spend 30-90 minutes per day talking to friends and people that I work with. In fact, the very first word my son ever said was, "Hello," which he said into a fake red plastic phone. So that tells you that he's seen me talk on the phone quite a bit.

Having a headset phone means that I can talk AND walk around and do stuff without getting that annoying crick in my neck that my cordless phone gives me. I treasure this phone. I use it every day. It's a constant reminder of the best birthday gift I ever received.

How about you? Do you have a favorite birthday or Christmas gift that you use every day, or almost every day? Maybe it's your hair dryer. Or your leather jacket. Or your DVD player. Or your Toyota.

What if I told you that there's an even better gift that you might not have found yet that you can also use every day. It's way more valuable than even your Toyota. But somehow it's ended up in a corner of your room, covered up by your jeans and last week's history notes on World War II.

It's your spiritual gift. What's a spiritual gift? A spiritual gift is a special talent or ability that God has given you to serve others. Let's unwrap that a little bit more. (Pardon the pun.)

1. All followers of Christ are given gifts. From the moment that you ask Jesus to take over your life and sit in the driver's seat, you are given spiritual gifts. Most folks have two or three that are more dominant than the rest, but no one person has all the gifts. Well, except Jesus, but that's because he was fully God and fully human. The Apostle Paul describes these different kinds of spiritual gifts in Romans 12:1-8 and 1 Corinthians 12:1-11 and 12: 27-31.

2. All the gifts are important. Sometimes we look at our pastor and assume that she is more important than we are. Or we figure the people who teach Sunday school are more special than those who clean up the kitchen. Instead, the Bible paints a different picture (as usual!). Paul writes more about the importance of all gifts in 1 Corinthians 12.

   You can easily enough see how this kind of thing works by looking no further than your own body…A body isn't just a single part blown up into something huge. It's all the different-but-similar parts arranged and functioning together…An enormous eye or a gigantic hand wouldn't be a body, but a monster. What we have is one body with many parts, each its proper size and in its proper place. No part is important on its own. Can you imagine Eye telling Hand, "Get lost; I don't need you"? Or, Head telling Foot, "You're fired; your job has been phased out"? As a matter of fact, in practice it works the other way — the "lower" the part, the more basic, and therefore necessary. You can live without an eye, for instance, but not without a stomach…If anything, you have more concern for the lower parts than the higher. If you had to choose, wouldn't you prefer good digestion to full-bodied hair? (I Cor. 12:12-24)" (Eugene Peterson, *The Message*, Colorado Springs, Colorado: NavPress Publishing Group, 1993, 357-358.)

   Paul's right. I mean, I love my hair and everything, but if push came to shove and I had to choose between my visible hair and my invisible intestines that let me eat Mexican food, I'll shave my head any day of the week. The behind-the-scenes gifts are just as important as the up-front gifts, even if they're not as visible.

3. All share the same purpose. The goal of the gifts isn't to look cool in front of your friends or to get your youth pastor to like you. Paul writes in Ephesians 4:11-13 that the ultimate goal of the gifts is to build up the body of Christ, meaning the church. Every time you use your spiritual gift and serve others, it's like going to the gym and working on your triceps. Not only do you get stronger, but your whole body benefits. So when you use your gift of mercy to visit someone who's bummed because their dad just took off, you benefit, your bummed friend benefits, and eventually the body benefits because more ministry happens.

So how do you know what gifts you have? Great question. We suggest a combination of three things.

1. Ask other people. Like we'll talk about in the next chapter on Friendship, you need other people to help you see reality. Your parents, siblings, friends, small group leader, or pastor might have some ideas on your gifts and talents.

2. Get experience. You might think you have the gift of evangelism, but you realize when you try it that you hate it and stink at it. That might mean you don't really have the gift. So start with what you're good at and what you enjoy.

3. Take a test. Hey, you're in luck. We've got a test for you.

✳ *Spiritual Gifts Test*

Hopefully by now you've read about spiritual gifts. Are you wondering what gifts you have to unwrap?

Do this: Grab a pencil, this book, and about 20 minutes and take the test below. Read the following statements one at a time. And then mark how true that is of you in the grid that follows on page 111.

1. I could be described as an "others-centered" person.

2. I enjoy giving hope to people who are hurting.

3. When people are in need, I enjoy having them in my home. I don't feel like they're crowding my space.

4. I have a prayer language which is a tongue that is unknown to me.

5. God has used me in a supernatural way to heal someone.

6. I have the ability to comfort those who are really depressed.

7. I see myself as a person who is very generous when it comes to giving money to others or my church.

8. My friends view me as a person who is wise.

9. I have expressed deep thoughts that have given insights to others.

10. I find it easy to trust God in difficult situations.

11. I would like to be a missionary.

12. It is pretty easy for me to tell nonbelievers about my relationship with Christ.

13. I have given others important messages that I felt came from God at the perfect time.

14. I enjoy explaining biblical truths to people.

15. I try to know people in a personal way so that we feel comfortable with each other.

16. I believe I know where I am going and other people seem to follow.

17. I can give others responsibilities for a task or project and help them accomplish it.

18. God's done some really cool stuff in people's lives through me.

19. I have heard someone speak in an unknown language and been able to interpret what he or she said.

20. I enjoy meeting the needs of others.

21. I am very compassionate to people who are hurting.

22. I enjoy having new people in my home. I like making them feel comfortable.

23. I have spoken in tongues.

24. I have prayed and seen God heal someone who was really sick or physically disabled.

25. I want to learn more about counseling so I can encourage others.

26. I really want to use my money wisely, knowing that God will direct my giving.

27. I believe God has given me the ability to make wise decisions.

28. I desire to really understand biblical truths.

29. I trust in God for supernatural miracles.

30. I feel comfortable when I'm around people of a different race, language, or culture.

31. I have the ability to direct conversations toward the gospel and the message of Christ.

32. I sometimes have the ability to reveal God's truth about the future.

33. I think I have what it takes to teach a Bible study or lead a small group discussion.

34. I would like the responsibilities that my pastor has.

35. I would enjoy leading, inspiring, and motivating others to become involved in God's word.

36. I am able to set goals and plan the most effective way to reach them.

37. God has used me to specifically perform miraculous signs and wonders.

38. God has shown me what someone was saying when he or she was speaking in tongues.

39. You'll frequently find me volunteering my time to help other people who have needs.

40. I would like to have a ministry with those who are needy.

41. I want my house to always be a place where people in need can come and find rest.

42. An unknown language comes to me when I'm at a loss for words during my prayer time.

43. As I've prayed, I've seen God heal others through me.

44. I enjoy seeing people respond to my encouraging words.

45. I am confident that God will take care of my needs when I give sacrificially and cheerfully.

46. I usually see clear solutions to complicated problems.

47. I have the ability to learn new insights on my own.

48. Others in my group see me as someone who is full of faith.

49. I adapt easily to new things.

50. I have prayed with other people as they have received Christ.

51. I have given messages that were judgments from God.

52. I am willing to spend extra time studying biblical principles in order to communicate them clearly to others.

53. I would like to be a pastor.

54. I have influenced others to complete a task or to find a biblical answer that helped their lives.

55. I enjoy learning about management issues and how organizations function.

56. God has performed humanly impossible miracles in my life.

57. I have interpreted tongues in such a way that it has blessed others.

58. I'm the type of person who likes to reach out to less fortunate people.

59. I would like to visit rest homes and other institutions where people are lonely and need visitors.

60. I enjoy providing food and housing to those in need.

61. Others have interpreted my unknown prayer language.

62. God seems to heal others through me.

63. I am known for the way I encourage others.

64. I am a cheerful giver of my money.

65. God has given me the ability to give clear counsel and advice to others.

66. I tend to use biblical insights when I share with others.

67. I find it pretty easy to pray really way-out prayers.

68. I have a strong desire to see people in other countries become followers of Christ.

69. I always think of new ways that I can share Christ with my non-Christian friends.

70. I desire to speak messages from God that will challenge people to change.

71. God has used my teaching to help others better understand what it means to be a Christian.

72. I can see myself taking responsibility for the spiritual growth of others.

73. When I'm in a group, I am usually the leader or I take the lead if no one else does.

74. While I'm pretty good at doing work myself, I like inviting others to help me and organizing what we all do.

75. I have witnessed God's miraculous power in and through my life.

76. God has used my gift of interpretation of tongues to speak a message to others.

This test is adapted from Jim Burns and Doug Fields' work, *The Word on Finding and Using Your Spiritual Gifts*, Gospel Light: Ventura, 1995, 195-201.

✳ Spiritual Gifts Test Grid

One at a time, read the statements on pages 108 to 110 and write your response next to the corresponding number below. Here are the possible responses:

3 = Totally like me
2 = Somewhat like me
1 = A little like me
0 = Not me at all

Then add up the four numbers you have recorded in each row and place the sum in the "total" column.

Value of Answers				Total	Gift
1 ___	20 ___	39 ___	58 ___	___	Service
2 ___	21 ___	40 ___	59 ___	___	Mercy
3 ___	22 ___	41 ___	60 ___	___	Hospitality
4 ___	23 ___	42 ___	61 ___	___	Tongues
5 ___	24 ___	43 ___	62 ___	___	Healing
6 ___	25 ___	44 ___	63 ___	___	Encouragement
7 ___	26 ___	45 ___	64 ___	___	Giving
8 ___	27 ___	46 ___	65 ___	___	Wisdom
9 ___	28 ___	47 ___	66 ___	___	Knowledge
10 ___	29 ___	48 ___	67 ___	___	Faith
11 ___	30 ___	49 ___	68 ___	___	Apostleship
12 ___	31 ___	50 ___	69 ___	___	Evangelism
13 ___	32 ___	51 ___	70 ___	___	Prophecy
14 ___	33 ___	52 ___	71 ___	___	Teaching
15 ___	34 ___	53 ___	72 ___	___	Pastoring
16 ___	35 ___	54 ___	73 ___	___	Leadership
17 ___	36 ___	55 ___	74 ___	___	Administration
18 ___	37 ___	56 ___	75 ___	___	Miracles
19 ___	38 ___	57 ___	76 ___	___	Interpretation

Now that you have a hunch about which gifts you might have, turn to the next page for a Crash Course on Using Your Gift.

A Crash Course on Using Your Gift

By now you have some glimmers of what your gifts might be. Now what do you do? Here are some ideas on things you can do with your gifts in the next few weeks. Frankly, you can probably come up with better ideas, but at least this will get you started.

Gift	Definition	Scripture	How to Use
Service	Identifying people's needs and then finding a way to meet them, often without letting others know what you're doing.	Romans 12:7	Ask your small group leader, youth pastor, or pastor if you can volunteer a few hours each week to help them. Choose one surprise chore to do for your parents each week. Give a friend or sibling a ride to their piano practice or soccer game.
Mercy	Feeling compassion toward others, especially those in need.	Romans 12:8	Serve in a retirement home or homeless shelter. Read some books or take some classes on counseling. Volunteer a few hours per week to help kids who are hurting at your church.
Hospitality	Warmly welcoming people into your life home, and room.	Romans 12:9-13	Invite a few kids who are new over to your house for snacks. Have a slumber party with your small group. Invite your small group leader, youth pastor or pastor over for dinner.
Tongues	Speaking in a language you have not heard, often while praying or while giving a message to others.	1 Corinthians 12:10, 28	Be open to speaking in tongues during your prayer times alone. When you walk into church services, ask God to make you open to how He wants to work through you.
Healing	Serving as a person through whom God heals.	1 Corinthians 12:9, 28	Pray for three people you know who have physical illnesses. Volunteer to pray with people who need healing after the next church service.
Encouragement	Sharing words of comfort or empowerment with others.	Romans 12:8	Write letters to 5 people you know who need encouragement. Buy an inexpensive, but meaningful, gift for an adult who you really appreciate. Spend 5 minutes telling your small group leader or pastor what you appreciate about them.
Giving	Contributing material resources both sacrificially and cheerfully.	Romans 12:8	Plan a money or toy drive for your youth group or church. Pray about giving some extra money to a church or charity this month. Decide not to buy anything new for yourself for the next 2 months and give the money you save to someone who really needs it.

Gift	Definition	Scripture	How to Use
Wisdom	Receiving insight from the Holy Spirit that can help others.	1 Corinthians 12:8	Spend extra time in Scripture study to make sure your ears are open to the Holy Spirit. Pray for friends who are in tricky situations and ask God to show you what to tell them.
Knowledge	Discovering and analyzing ideas and information to help others.	1 Corinthians 12:8	Ask an adult about a problem that's really bugging them and see if you can help them figure out what to do. Design a Bible reading plan for the next few months so that you stay in touch with the Holy Spirit.
Faith	Having extraordinary confidence in God's plan and work.	1 Corinthians 12:9	Identify three God-sized tasks and ask God to start working. Find someone who's struggling with their faith and share some of what God has done for you.
Apostleship	Sharing the gospel in new cultures and environments	Ephesians 4:11-13	Pray about doing a cross-cultural short-term missions trip this summer. With the help of some adults, go downtown and distribute sandwiches to people who live on the street.
Evangelism	Sharing the gospel with unbelievers.	1 Corinthians 12:9, 28	Pray for three friends who don't know Jesus yet. Ask your closest non-Christian friend if you could share about your most important friendship. Show a provocative movie to some friends and lead a discussion afterwards.
Prophecy	Communicating a message from God to others.	1 Corinthians 12:10, 28	Ask God to show you what to say and stay humble in the meantime. Pray for a friend who is struggling and see if God shows you anything to share with them.
Teaching	Communicating a message that helps others learn.	1 Corinthians 12:28	Look for some younger kids and start teaching them. Ask if you can teach at your youth group sometime. Help your youth pastor figure out what to talk about in the next few months.

Gift	Definition	Scripture	How to Use
Pastoring	Shepherding a group.	Ephesians t4:11-13	Ask your youth pastor or pastor if you can hang out with them for a few hours every week as they do their normal stuff. Volunteer to lead or co-lead a small group.
Leadership	Influencing a group toward a specific purpose.	Romans 12:8	Help design a vision statement for your small group or youth group. Read through Paul's epistles and write down the leadership qualities that you want in your own life.
Administration	Understanding goals and knowing how to organize others to reach them.	1 Corinthians 12:28	Take on a project at church and then organize a team to help you. Ask your youth pastor if you can brainstorm some goals together and then figure out how to meet them.
Miracles	Receiving God's power to perform powerful acts.	1 Corinthians 12:10, 28	Look around for some God-sized needs and start praying for them. Read the book of Matthew and notice what happens every time God heals someone.
Interpretation	Translating a message in tongues into everyday language.	1 Corinthians 12:10, 30	Next time you walk into church, pray that God will make you open to whatever He wants. Read the book of Acts and jot down what happens when people speak in tongues.

Think about it...

* According to the test, what spiritual gifts do you have?
* Do you agree with this, or disagree? Why?
* What ideas do you have about how you can use these gifts?
* What might happen if you do? Oh wait, let us answer that one. You might just be changed by Christ to change the world around you.

School Daze

Where do you spend the most time, at least while you're awake? Probably your school. When it comes to impacting your school, lots of times we feel like these girls:

Sherri

Why is it that I can act all Christian at church, but when it comes to school, it's like I shove my relationship with God in my locker?

My friend, Alan, is really having a hard time. His mom is leaving his step-dad, so Alan thinks he's going to have to move and start going to a new school. When he told me this at lunch, I wanted to say so badly, "I'll pray for you." And maybe even, "Can we pray about this right now?" If I was at church talking to Alan, I'd totally do it. But when I'm at school, it's like I'm afraid or something. Afraid of what Alan will think. Afraid that he'll laugh at me, or think I'm a dork or something.

Betsy

If I hear my youth pastor talk about "impacting my school" one more time, I think I will throw up. I'm so sick of him talking about how proud he is of Kelly for leading a campus Bible study at her school, and of Colin for praying with the football team. We can't all be Billy Grahams. I just want to be a normal student.

Amy

Today is Bible study day at lunch. I kind of like it, but I wish it wasn't so often. I always go grab hamburgers with my friends at lunch, so today I'm going to have to make up some excuse about why I'm not going. I know I should tell them that I'm going to Bible study instead. But that sounds so lame. I've used the ole' "meeting with a teacher" excuse too much lately. I'll have to come up with something new.

Think about it:

* What, if anything, do these girls have in common?
* How do you think their self-image might be influencing the way they view the reaction of their friends and school to their Christianity?
* Which of these girls is most like you: Sherri, Betsy or Amy? Why?
* Which of these girls is least like you? Why?
* Lots of times teenagers don't share about their faith at school because they're afraid, ashamed, or apathetic (maybe thinking a little bit more about themselves than about their friends who need Christ).
* What do you think he would say to Sherri, Betsy, or Amy? To you? Why?
* Describe aloud the kind of Christian you want to be at school. In prayer, ask God to mold you and shape you to become that Christian.
* What one thing can you do this week to more fully live out Jesus' words?

Ways to Change Your Campus

Tell a friend in crisis that you're praying for them.

Ask a teacher if there's anything you can do to help them. And then do it.

Next time you study history around the time Jesus was born, ask your teacher if you can make a special presentation on the life of Christ. Everybody agrees that he was a real live person.

Join a service club. Or maybe start one yourself.

Ask a few friends if they'd like to hear about the most important thing in your life. Some night over dinner or coffee, share about your life before you started your relationship with Christ, as well as after.

Pray every day for 3 friends to come to know Christ.

Next time you go to a party where there is alcohol and someone asks you why you're not drinking, give them the real reason.

Invite your friends to a thought-provoking movie, and then grab dessert afterwards to talk about it.

Next time you're in crisis, share your true feelings with a friend, and how you're trying to meet Jesus and trust him in the midst of them.

Invite a few other Christian friends to pray with you at lunch one day a week.

Next time you get a chance to do a book report, try using a Christian book.

Invite a few friends to come to your church with you.

Give a friend a CD that's either got Christian music on it, or music that asks lots of great questions about life. Talk with them about it a few weeks later.

Pray for Christian teachers or administrators who are at your school.

Give your friends Christmas cards that explain the REAL meaning of Christmas.

The next time your small group or church hosts a service activity (a missions trip, homeless feeding, convalescent home visit), bring along a few friends.

Leave a Bible in your backpack or car. You never know what conversation might start.

Follow My Lead

If you're serious about changing the world, you're going to start influencing others. How do you know you're going to influence them to do the right thing? What if you do things that take people down the wrong path?

These are questions that every leader deals with. Including one of the most famous leaders in the Bible, Paul. But while Paul encouraged people to follow his lead, he ultimately wanted people to fall in love with and follow Christ.

Here's how he explains it to the people in Corinth:

"Follow my example as I follow the example of Christ" (1 Corinthians 11:1). Now some might think Paul was being proud or arrogant in asking people to imitate him. But keep in mind who Paul ultimately wanted people to imitate. Jesus, remember?

How about you? What kind of an example are you? What would happen if people followed your lead? How would that make you feel about yourself?

On the left side of this sheet, make a list of all the things about yourself that you would want people to imitate. If they imitated you, they'd be imitating Jesus. It might be the way you treat your little brother, or the way you work hard at soccer practice, or the way you're trying to be nice to less popular kids at school.

Now on the right side of this sheet, make a list of all the things about yourself that you wouldn't want people to imitate. If people copied your example, you'd be embarrassed. We probably don't need to give you any ideas here. You've probably thought of some yourself by now.

Circle one thing from the left side of the line that you want to make sure you keep doing this week. Now circle one thing from the right that you want to try to stop doing this week.

Great. Now ask God to help you experience his grace so that you can be the person you want to be.

College 101

College is a great way to learn stuff that will help you change your world. Although college isn't for everybody, it just might be for you. Don't let your insecurities keep you from going. Whether you come from a long line of college-bound siblings, or whether you're the first in your family to think about applying, here's a chance to test your college IQ.

1. A bachelor's degree is

A. What every single male gets when he finishes college.

B. What you get after finishing four years at a college or university.

C. What you get if you graduate with more than a 3.5 g.p.a.

2. A junior college is

A. A two-year school where you can take a lot of basic courses and save truckloads of money.

B. A school for people who are 5'6" or shorter.

C. A school for rich kids who are named after their parents.

3. A fraternity is

A. A club for girls.

B. A club for guys.

C. A really long time.

4. What's the difference between a quarter and a semester?

A. A quarter is 25 cents, and a semester is 75 cents.

B. A quarter lasts 10 weeks, while a semester lasts 15 weeks.

C. A semester lasts 10 weeks, while a quarter lasts 15 weeks.

5. If you want to keep going to school after you finish your bachelor's degree, you will likely try to get a degree called a

A. Master's degree.

B. Help-I-Owe-Tons-Of-Money degree.

C. Third degree.

6. Who lives in a dormitory?

A. Students.

B. Rodents.

C. Both of the above.

7. How many times should you take the S.A.T. test to get into college?

A. As many times as that cute guy in your math class takes it.

B. As many times as you can. Generally, your scores improve the more you take it.

C. Once, and only once.

8. If you stay up until 6 a.m. to finish a paper, that is called

A. A huge hangover.

B. A major rager.

C. An all nighter.

9. Your first year of college is called you

A. Rookie year.

B. Junior year.

C. Freshman year.

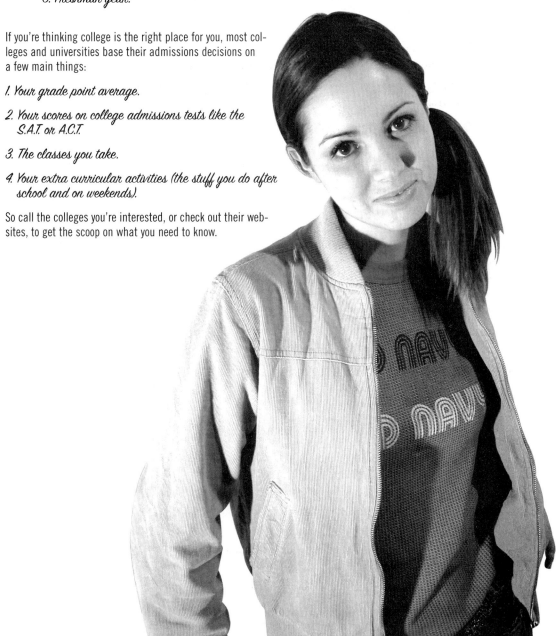

If you're thinking college is the right place for you, most colleges and universities base their admissions decisions on a few main things:

1. Your grade point average.

2. Your scores on college admissions tests like the S.A.T. or A.C.T.

3. The classes you take.

4. Your extra curricular activities (the stuff you do after school and on weekends).

So call the colleges you're interested, or check out their websites, to get the scoop on what you need to know.

Answers:
1. B **2.** A **3.** B **4.** B **5.** A **6.** A or C, depending on the dormitory. **7.** B **8.** C. **9.** C.

Real Girls
MTV to You and Me

We all have those times when we feel like we're no good at anything. What should we do when we feel that way? Call a friend? Eat all the chocolate we can find? Go shopping? Maybe. Or maybe instead, we should try some of what these girls recommend.

What steps do you take to get out of the "failure" blahs?

Elaine W.: "Talk to someone, like a good friend, who you know will help. Dish out your feelings. Spoil yourself—do the things you love to do. Somehow make yourself feel more special."

Searcy C.: "The only advice I can give is to make a list of all the things you think you're good at. Then, when you feel depressed or lonely, you can look at that list and feel better. And most of all…PRAY."

Erica M.: "I'd try reading the Bible, especially the Psalms. Hang out with someone who can cheer you up and make you laugh. Learn from your mistakes by figuring out what you'd do differently next time."

Brittany H.: "My mom always told me, 'God doesn't make junk.' Sure, failure comes into everyone's life, but there's always something you're good at. Remember all the successes you've already had."

Emily B.: "Talk to those who are closest to you and see the kind of impact you have made on their lives. If you have touched even one other person, you're not a failure."

Kathy W.: "Try not to dwell on your failures, but rather focus on some of your successes. I know it's hard to do, but if you can do it, it brings a new perspective."

Emily C.: "Go to God. Even though it's hard to do sometimes, he is the only one who can fill the void inside of you. And don't keep it all inside. Talk with friends or someone older than you. Chances are that they've been where you are and can relate."

Christy G.: "I'd recommend reading your Bible. The Psalms always do the trick for me."

Macall R.: "Talk to someone who is always encouraging. My mom never thinks I'm a failure, so when things are bad, I go to her."

mirror mirror

by Kara Powell and Kendall Payne

Food&Eating
How Hungry Are You?

* ## QUESTIONS ABOUT FOOD
Forget What You Thought You Knew

* ## CONTROL
The Sequel

* ## HOW DO YOU RATE
Living In Your Own Universe

Plus: A Portrait of a Winning Gymnast

*How Hungry Are You?

Imagine that you are a recovering alcoholic surrounded by pictures of beer. Your kitchen is somehow always full of wine, brandy, and vodka. Friends casually call you and ask you if you want to go out to a restaurant for a drink. For them, going out for a drink is no big deal. For you, it threatens to pull you down a slippery slope toward despair and depression. And to top it all off, you have a rare genetic disease that requires you to drink a glass of red wine three times per day. All this while you're trying to get over your addiction to alcohol.

Sound far fetched? Well, if we're talking about alcohol, it is (especially the part about the rare genetic disease).

But if we're talking about food, maybe it's not so far off. For most girls and women (maybe even all), food is not a neutral issue. Food has the power to make us feel either strong and healthy or guilty and worthless. In short, there is a strong connection between the way we feel about food and the way we feel about ourselves. And since there's no way to stay alive without eating, we've got to come to terms with it.

There are two kinds of eating. The first is healthy eating. That's when you're hungry, and you do something about it. And what you do about it is generally pretty good for you (you choose fruit over cookies, chicken over candy bars), and you stop when you're full.

The other kind of eating is emotional eating. That's when you're not really that physically hungry, but you're emotionally hungry. You feel angry, lonely, or maybe even ecstatic, and to comfort your pain or to celebrate your joy, you reach for that bag of tortilla chips and that jar of salsa. Or peanut butter swirl ice cream. Or a batch of uncooked cookie dough. Or _____ (you fill in the blank with your own favorite comfort food).

Let's face it: there's not a girl or woman alive who hasn't done some emotional eating. The question is: how much are you doing? Is it a once a month thing, or a once you get home from school every day thing?

The problem is that the more you emotionally eat, the worse you feel about yourself. The worse you feel about yourself, the more you emotionally eat. And so you get caught in a vicious cycle that leaves you feeling more like Miss Piggy than Miss America.

As you'll see in this chapter, all sorts of feelings go hand in hand with food: control, failure, safety, and fear, just to name a few. But if you read carefully, you'll see the thread that weaves it all together: there is a God who is far bigger than that triple scoop hot fudge sundae with extra nuts on top. And He loves you more than you can imagine.

Cheetos and...Frosting
By Kendall

Food! Oh we love it and hate it! One of my favorite authors is a woman named Anne Lamott. Her book *Traveling Mercies* describes, in a chapter titled "Hunger," her lifelong battle with food and eating. Below is an excerpt from this chapter. In it Anne has just begun seeing Rita, a specialist in eating disorders, because she suffered from bulimia for many years.

Several weeks later, during one of our sessions, Rita asked me what I'd had for breakfast. "Cereal," I said.

"And were you hungry when you ate?"

"What do you mean?" I asked.

"I mean, did you experience hunger, and then make breakfast?"

"I don't really understand what you're asking," I said.

"Let me put it this way," she said. "Why did you have breakfast?"

"Oh! I see," I said. "I had breakfast because it was break-fast time."

"But were you hungry?"

I stared at her a moment. "Is this a trick question?" I asked

"No," she said. "I just want to know how you know it's time to eat."

"I know it's time to eat because it's mealtime," I said. "It's morning, so I eat breakfast, or it's midday, so I eat lunch. And so on."

To make a long story ever so slightly shorter, she finally asked me what it felt like when I was hungry, and I could not answer. I asked her to explain what it felt like when she was hungry, and she described a sensation in her stomach of emptiness, an awareness of appetite.

So for the next week, my assignment was to notice what it felt like when I was hungry. It was so strange. I was once again the world's oldest toddler. I walked around peering down as if to look inside my stomach, and I paid attention until I was able to isolate this feeling in my stomach, a gritchy kind of emptiness, like a rat was scratching at the door, wanting to be let in.

"Wonderful," Rita said, and then gave me my next assignment: first, to notice when I was hungry, and then—this blew my mind—to feed myself!

So I'd feel the scratchy emptiness in my belly, and I'd mention to myself that I seemed hungry. And then I'd ask myself, in a deeply maternal way, what I felt like eating.

"Well, actually, I feel like some Cheeto's," I might say. So I'd go and buy a bag of Cheeto's, put some in a bowl, and eat them. It was amazing. Then I'd check in with myself: "Do you want some more?" I'd ask. "No," I'd say. "But don't throw them out."

I had been throwing food out or wetting it in the sink since I was fourteen, ever since my first diet. Every time I broke down and ate forbidden foods, I would throw out or wet what I'd left uneaten, because each time I was about to start over and be good again.

"I'm hungry," I'd say to myself. "I'd like some frosting."

"OK"

"And some Cheetos."

So I'd have some frosting and some Cheetos for breakfast. I'd eat for a while. Then I'd check with myself, kindly: "More?"

"Not now," I'd say. "But don't wet them. I might want some more later."

I ate frosting and Cheetos for weeks.

Each of us has a remarkable ability to self-deceive about food. Anne's ability was so great that she had totally blocked out her body's hunger messages. She had to consciously remind herself to pick up on her body's signals indicating she was hungry. Food is not our enemy, but our wrong attitudes toward food, unchallenged in our heart, may well be. In this chapter, gain a healthy perspective on food, eating and fitness.

*Control
The Sequel

By Cindi

Ginny could totally relate. It turns out that she'd been seeing a counselor herself about eating issues. She was a lot like me—she seemed together on the outside and everyone congratulated her for losing weight, but inside she felt out of control. The very food that she was trying to control was now controlling her.

Ginny's counselor encouraged her to eat something at every meal. If she ever skipped a meal, she might start skipping more meals. Even if she just had a small salad, she needed to eat something.

She asked me if I would make that same commitment. I said I would.

Then as we were walking our bikes to class, she said, "Since we have the same class every Tuesday and Thursday at 1:15, how about if we meet for lunch at 12:45 on both of these days? That way we can share about how we're doing and pray for each other."

Ginny was super busy, so I never expected that she'd be able to make that much time for me. I was so honored that she cared that much. I said, "You bet. See you on Thursday at 12:45."

We met every Tuesday and Thursday all semester. At times, we had lots to talk about. But sometimes we just sat and nibbled on our lunches. Sometimes we prayed, other times we cried, and sometimes we even laughed.

Just like I promised Ginny, I also ate three meals a day. And slowly but surely, thanks to God's help, and to Ginny's, my life got more back to normal. Instead of being my enemy, food became my friend.

For several years after college, I kept a framed picture of me and Ginny on my desk, just to remind me of the meaning of true friendship. I haven't talked with her for years, but I'm forever grateful to her. Without her, I might have developed a full-blown eating disorder. Without her, I'm pretty sure I would have been trapped in feelings of self-hatred and insecurity.

Don't get me wrong: I still have down days, and every once in a while, I'm tempted to skip a meal. But to this day, I haven't. After all, I promised Ginny.

Portrait of a Winning Gymnast

By Gina Bolenbaugh

I don't know exactly how it happened. It's not that I ever took a clean sweep, but I was always up there—on the awards stand—at least once or twice. What went wrong this time?

I found myself sitting with my gymnastics teammates waiting for my name to be called, but it never was. The noise of the applause was drowned out by the ringing in my ears. My face was hot, and all I heard over and over again was the name of this little girl who looked more like an 11-year-old than a high school student. She won just about everything.

During the next week, my thoughts revolved around this little girl, and I wondered how she could be so small. I equated her size with her ability to win, her physical perfection with her competitive edge.

How did I get so big? When did "I let myself go?" I lost because I was fat. I was a slob. If I lost some weight, I could run faster, flip higher, and land easier. My coach agreed. My parents agreed. And I became consumed by the question, what do I need to do to lose this weight?

My mom helped me eat more carefully. We read content labels endlessly. As I lost weight, my dad commented on how fit and slender I looked. My teammates encouraged me, and helped me scheme. Evelyn advised, "Tell them you ate at my house today and just go to your room." Jenny cut in, "If you have to eat, you can always just throw up – it's not that hard after the first few times."

I met positive feedback everywhere I turned; coaches, parents, teammates were more proud of me than before. I looked more like the girls I competed against, and the girls in the magazines, the models on the runways, and even the starlets on the screen. I felt totally in control, powerful, sleek and strong.

I weighed in at practice, at first every other week, soon every week, then every day…then before and after practice…then when I got up, when I got home, and whenever I was around a scale…when no one was around… I just got on. The scale was like a carnival ride that I couldn't resist. I always felt the same when I got off: woozy, unreal, wondering why I had eaten that last bite—and how I could lose more weight.

Even though it's been a few years since then, a lot has changed, but much remains the same. I still stare at my body when I get out of the
shower. Every angle, every ounce, every pinch is analyzed.

I think of the other girls. They are all smaller than me, all of them better than me, all of them in control, working harder, winning.

My own voice screams at me in my head. "Stupid, stupid, stupid! Why did you eat that bagel this morning? Why couldn't you just be satisfied with grapes? You had to reach for more! Now you'll have to go running after practice until you burn every calorie you put into your fat pig-like body."

Eating equals failure. I am embarrassed to eat in front of others, afraid that they will see my weakness.

When will I achieve the perfection I strain for? What does the perfect girl look like? I'll know it when I get there, I lie to myself. Deep down I know I'll never be there, but I will kill myself trying.

There is still a constant pain in the pit of my stomach. All I know is this pain. But I've learned to endure it. I feel guilty when I eat, guilty when I vomit, ashamed in a leotard, guilty when my routines are off, angry when I don't win. I punish myself. I hate myself and I can't do anything right. I don't deserve anything good. I don't deserve to eat.

Continued on next page…

✳ *Think about it...*

✳ *What is your first reaction to this girl's story?*

✳ *What do you think about this girl's food limits and weight loss goals? Why?*

✳ *Do you set goals about how much you will, or won't eat? Is that a good thing? Why?*

✳ *How about exercise—do you have goals for working out also? How do you feel if you don't meet those?*

✳ *Think about your friends—do guys care as much as girls about exercise and food? Why?*

✳ *Is it OK to try and eat healthy and to watch one's weight? When does this become a problem?*

✳ *If you ate totally healthy, how would your life be different?*

Q&A on Food
with Pam Erdman

Is it possible to have a totally healthy relationship with food? Is it possible to like your body and feel good about yourself? According to Pam Erdman, the answer to both questions is "Yes," but it sure isn't easy. As a marriage, family and child therapist, she's spent 20 years meeting with girls to talk about food, their bodies, and the way the two go together.

We recently had a chance to ask her a bunch of questions—the kinds of questions you would want to ask—and she gave us some surprising answers. Whether you struggle with food, or know someone who does (add the two together and you pretty much cover everyone), her answers will open your eyes to the truth about food.

What is an eating disorder?

An eating disorder is what happens when your relationship with food is distorted enough that it impacts the quality of your life. Almost all of us have struggles with food, but when food starts to profoundly impact your social, emotional, and spiritual life, you might have an eating disorder.

What are the main types of eating disorders?

Well, there are four types. The first two, anorexia and bulimia, get a lot of attention in the media. Anorexia is actually pretty rare because technically a girl has to starve herself until she is 25% below her ideal body weight. A girl is bulimic when she binges on a lot of food, like 1,600 or 2,000 calories in one sitting. Then she purges, or gets rid of, the food, through vomiting, laxatives, drugs like speed, or excessive exercising.

The third isn't as well known. It's called bulimerexia, and it's like a combination between bulimia and anorexia. A girl doesn't have to be 25% below her ideal body weight, like in anorexia, but she is probably pretty thin. And like a bulimic, she spends a lot of time and energy trying to figure out how to stay that way. She's probably pretty controlled and disciplined, so she's most likely to turn to excessive exercising as a way to get rid of the calories she's eaten.

The fourth is compulsive overeating. It's actually probably the most common of all of them. This girl likely doesn't exercise much, and overeats because she doesn't know how to handle her emotions. Her weight is like a yo-yo—it will go up and down—but she's usually at least 30 pounds overweight.

You've mentioned exercising quite a bit already. Isn't that a good thing to do?

Yes, it is, but for too many teenage girls, exercise is part of the mind games they play with their food. Instead of playing sports like soccer, swimming, or gymnastics for fun, girls with unhealthy attitudes toward food view them as ways to purge, or get rid of, the calories they've eaten.

What about dieting? Is that OK to do?

Well, moderate dieting isn't an actual eating disorder, but the bottom line is that diets don't work. You might lose weight for a while, but then you almost always gain it back. Plus you usually put on even more weight long-term

What causes eating disorders?

The number one cause of eating disorders is the need to control. Girls who feel internally, emotionally or spiritually out of control might look to food as something that can be easily controlled. Girls who don't have the skills to deal with their feelings might do the same thing.

Continued on next page...

But there are also other causes. Some girls fear growing up, others fear their emerging sexuality. Plus girls' families are part of the equation. Families that are either chaotic or super controlling might make a girl want to have some control of her own.

Families that have super-high expectations and put a lot of pressure on daughters might make a girl more likely to have an eating disorder. Or families that lack emotional support and don't help their daughters deal with their feelings often have daughters who struggle with food.

✳ Isn't it enough for a mom or dad to compliment their daughter on how she looks?

Well, that's a start, but it's not enough. Moms who say their daughter is beautiful one minute, but then criticize their own bodies the next minute, send mixed messages. The girl hears that her mom doesn't like her own body so therefore she can't like hers either. Plus parents who are constantly criticizing other people's bodies might send their daughters the message that anything less than a perfect body is unacceptable.

✳ Are girls today more, or less, likely to develop eating disorders now than ten or twenty years ago?

I think more. Expectations are rising for girls. Many families focus on success, which boils down to appearance and achievement. Girls who are under a lot of pressure about their looks, grades, or sports but who don't have a lot of emotional support are eating disorders waiting to happen.

✳ Are there particular ages at which a girl is most likely to have an eating disorder?

Yes, there are two main stages of life that are danger zones. The first is when a girl is 12 or 13 and entering puberty. The second is when she begins college. She has left her family, and she compensates for the separation by trying to control her food.

✳ We've been talking a lot about girls. What about guys? Do they get eating disorders?

Yes, they do, but not as much as girls. But I think it's going to rise soon. More and more men are moving toward body building, exercise, and body sculpting. Plus men tend to be more overweight. Add these up and you get someone who's likely to struggle with food.

✳ How do I know if a friend is struggling with an eating disorder?

Well, there are lots of signs. Here are a few:

✳ A girl will change her behavior. For instance, she might have previously loved going out for pizza and movies, but now she chooses to stay home instead. A girl with an eating disorder often ends up isolated. Like someone who is depressed, she would rather go home and sleep than be with people.

✳ She might develop odd eating behaviors and rituals. She doesn't eat like before. She eats way more or way less.

✳ She wears baggy clothes to cover her body.

✳ She sudden gains or loses a lot of weight.

✳ She talks about her weight A LOT.

✳ She describes herself as "fat" when she's really pretty thin.

✳ She lies about food. She might say that "I already ate" when you know she skipped breakfast and lunch.

Continued on next page...

What should I do if I think a friend has an eating disorder?

Talk to her and let her know you're concerned about her. Ask her to talk to a parent or an adult that she trusts. Volunteer to go with her if she'd like.

What if she won't talk with an adult? Should I tell her parents myself?

Tell your own parent(s) first. Together, figure out what to do. Or you can leave an anonymous note with a small group leader, school counselor, or youth pastor, asking their advice.

Pam, when you're counseling a girl who has an eating disorder, what are you hoping to do?

First, I want to help them get honest. I want to create a safe place where they can talk about their attitudes toward food. Next, we talk about why they might be eating and acting like they are. Third, I try to get to the emotions behind the behaviors. We try to figure out if there's a better way to deal with those feelings than starving themselves or exercising.

Besides going to counseling, what are some tangible things that a girl who's struggling with food can do?

She should start journaling. Journaling is a powerful way to record our inner feelings, and how we feel about ourselves. Plus she should meditate on Scripture. She needs to know how much God loves and cares about her. She might want to get into a support group, either at her church or at a place like Overeaters Anonymous, which often has free support groups for teens. Finally, she could contact her doctor, local school or church to find out more about how to get some personal and professional counseling.

Comfort

July 7

Food. It's my refuge. It's my safe place. Whenever I feel tired, stressed, bored, overwhelmed, and even happy, I am drawn to it. It makes me feel better. When I have plenty of food, I feel warm and safe.

July 23

I don't let myself ever get to the point of hunger. After school, before dinner, after dinner, when my homework is done, WHENEVER, I get comfort from those chips and Snickers bars. I keep some food in my room. I hide it in my bottom dresser drawer so that my mom and sisters won't eat it.

July 27

I think I'm addicted to sweets. If I don't have something sweet every day, I feel deprived and unsatisfied. I tell myself that I "deserve" whatever sweet I am trying to feed myself. Where is God's discipline in my life? Where is the source of my pain? Lord, I ask for your strength today that I might resist the strong pull of food in my life.

August 6

What is it that makes me overeat? Maybe it's because…

* My mom and step-dad have always used food to medicate themselves when times were tough.

* Around our house, we "eat our plate clean."

* As a little girl, I was punished for not finishing food.

* We celebrated with food. Report cards meant ice cream. Soccer games meant pizza.

* In elementary school, I was afraid of not having enough food. I remember the strong feelings of hunger at lunches and after school.

What am I going to do? It's hopeless. I can't beat it.

August 18

I think about food constantly. What did I eat? Did I eat too much? What will I have at the next meal? How will I reward myself with food? I plan ahead about what to eat but then give into temptation when I walk into the kitchen. I resolve every night that the next day will be different—but it isn't.

August 29

After reading over my last few entries, I'm starting to see patterns. I eat to feel good about myself. Because money and food were so scarce when I was a little girl, I thought a lot about food, and tried to hoard it. Today my parents have more than enough money for food. I don't need to worry about my next meal or gorging now because I don't know when I'll get to eat next. I can leave food on my plate. I don't have to eat everything NOW. I can wait until another day. I don't need to celebrate or pamper myself with food.

September 6

My most difficult times of the day are in the afternoon and early evening after I finish my homework. I get bored. I get sad. I get tired. I get weak.

September 20

I read Luke 4:4 today. It says, "But Jesus told him (Satan), 'No! The Scriptures say, 'People need more than bread for life.'" Hmmm… Lord, is this saying to me that I need more in my life than food? Or perhaps, Jesus would like me to know today that he has so much more to give me if and when food takes a lower place in my life. Jesus was able to resist temptation by abiding in the Father and quoting scripture. He quoted TRUTH to Satan and then Satan could not get him on that issue.

Lord, today, help me to use scripture to combat the temptations of food. Help me to abide in you today—sticking close so that I can hear, know and understand your truth.

September 22

I read Psalm 63 today. I don't know why. I'm supposed to still be reading Luke. Psalm 63:5 says, "You satisfy me more than the richest of foods. I will praise you with songs of joy."

This last verse snuck up on me. I actually went to write down another verse and this is the one I wrote. I didn't even know what I was writing until the end. Thank you Lord for reconfirming in my life the need for YOU to be number one. Forgive me again… for turning to food first—not running toward your feet to be satisfied. So I run to you with open arms this morning—crying out to my daddy.

Think about it...

* How would you describe Amy's attitude toward food?

* Do you ever run to food for comfort? If so, when are you most likely to do it?

* Amy grew up being scared that she wouldn't have enough food, so she had to eat it when she could. How has your past affected the way you view food?

* What truth do you need to remember about food today?

* When God is number one in your life, as Amy wrote in her last journal entry, how will that change your view of food?

Did you know...

* If you think about it, eating disorders are some of the hardest struggles to overcome. Alcoholics can avoid bars, drug addicts can avoid drugs, but someone recovering from an eating disorder can't avoid food.

* "Me, I see me, my disgustingly fat body blown out of proportion. The shower is running, the mirror is foggy, I am on my knees and my hair is back. I bend over the toilet, cold, white, unyielding. It is strong, my stability into which everything falls. My nails are chipped and peeling in places. I notice their imperfect polish as I see the rim around the edge of the bowl. Over I bend and shove my fingers back."

   From "Me, I See Me" by Lorel, in Sara Shandler's *Ophelia Speaks* (New York: Harper Perennial, 1999), 19.

* In a telephone poll of 1,000 women conducted by *People* magazine in 2000, when asked "Would you rather have Calista Flockhart's body or Camryn Manheim's?" 35% answered Calista's, and 43% answered Camryn's. Which would you have answered?

   "How Do I Look?" *People*, September 4, 2000, 117.

* Aerobic activity gets your heart pumping faster and more efficiently as your blood circulates. Workouts that raise a sweat can release endorphins and create a natural high, thus making you feel better about yourself. So next time you're having a "fat day," maybe you follow Elaine's advice and throw on those athletic shoes.

* The single largest group of high school students who consider or attempt suicide are girls who think they're overweight.

   Abby Ellin, "Dad, Do You Think I Look Too Fat?,"New York Times, September 17, 2000.

* "Sadly, how I feel about my body often dictates my mood. Like many girls, I don't really feel good about myself unless I'm feeling skinny. If I look in the mirror and all I can see is the fat on my thighs, then I'll usually feel negative for the rest of the day."

   Christie Schweer, "Never Thin Enough," *Campus Life*, September/October 2002.

How Do You Rate?

Are you the kind of girl who always compares herself to the height/ weight charts in the doctor's office? Are you always trying to figure out whether you weigh more or less than your friends?

Do this: Try this test. How do you rate in comparison with some of America's hottest actresses and a model?

Sarah Jessica Parker is 5'4" tall and weighs 100 pounds.

Jennifer Aniston is 5'5" and weighs 112 pounds.

Kate Moss stands at 5'6" but weights only 105 pounds.

To get a general idea of how you compare to these famous femmes, add 5 pounds for every inch that you're taller than them. For example, if you want to compare yourself to Sarah Jessica Parker, but you're 5'6", then add 10 pounds to her weight because you're two inches taller. If you want to compare yourself to Kate Moss but are 5'2", then subtract 20 pounds from her weight because you're four inches shorter. By the way, in Kate Moss standards, that would bring you to 85 pounds.

So how are you feeling about yourself? Do you fit in Kate Moss' world, or could you squeeze into Jennifer Aniston's jeans? To find out more, read the rest of this article printed upside down on this page.

Here's a bigger question: WHY DO YOU CARE?

Seriously, when it comes to body size, there's always someone who is smaller, thinner or more muscular than you. Even if you feel good because you can match up with Jennifer Aniston, you will probably never reach the land of Kate Moss. In fact, you could die trying.

If you use your body and the food you put into your body as the test for how you feel about yourself, you will always flunk. Even if you pass for a week or two, someone thinner comes along and ruins the curve.

Think about it...

* Why is it that you compare yourself to the height/weight charts? How does it make you feel?

* On a scale of 1-10, with 10 = really eager and 1=not caring a bit, how eager were you to compare yourself with famous models and actresses? Why?

* Do you think it's true that "Even if you feel good because you can match up with Jennifer Aniston, you will probably never reach the land of Kate Moss?" Why?

* What do you think this means: "In fact, you could die trying?"

Healthy Glow and a Healthy Body:
Myths or Reality?

You want to look your best. Looking your best involves more than just your physical appearance. The healthier the inside, the more confident we can be and wha-la!, the healthy glow. One of the best ways to get healthy hair, bright eyes, and clear skin is to eat a healthy balance of foods all day. Here is a list of myths many of us believe…and keys to a healthy body and a healthy glow:

MYTH #1
I am stuck with this body!

Wrong. You have more power than you know. All habits can be changed, and changed forever. If you can maintain a new way of eating, thinking, and exercising for even a month or two, you will establish a habit and are more likely to make this a lifelong success story. Those individuals who are able to stop bad habits and develop healthy ones find that a slow change is the one that lasts.

MYTH #2
Eating breakfast is optional…and makes me feel fat all day!

On the contrary, the first meal of your day gets your metabolism kicking. Your metabolism is your body's system of burning calories. Calories in the body are stored and used to feed muscles to perform any and all functions of the body. And first thing in the morning, your body is ready to burn some calories. True that excessive calories get stored in the body in the form of cellulite to be used later. But a balanced breakfast is the least likely meal of the day to make you fat.

MYTH #3
Muscles will only make me look fat!

The more muscle, the more calories needed to sustain that muscle. That means that if you have muscle, even when you are inactive you are burning more calories. Exercise, exercise, exercise! It doesn't have to be rigorous, just enough to get the heart rate higher than when you are resting. Maybe walk instead of drive, ride a bike instead of taking the bus, or start a sport with friends. Three times a week is all it takes. Bulky muscle may make you feel "big", but well-toned muscles will do a world of good for your body.

MYTH #4
The scale is my friend!

This one may be true if you have certain medical conditions, but generally speaking…stay away from the scale. It can only bring you down, especially if you have just started exercising. Muscle weighs more than fat, so even if you are exchanging muscle for fat and changing your shape, the scale will be discouraging. A good rule of thumb is to go by how your clothes feel and fit on the body. Don't let that piece of metal break your confidence.

MYTH #5
Skipping meals will help me lose weight!

Although it is true that lowering caloric intake does help you slim down, there are some things you should know about eating for success. You should be eating several smaller meals throughout the day. Snacking on the right foods is the key to success.

If you go more than five hours (with the exception of nighttime) without eating, then your body may not be getting enough calories to operate properly. Metabolism begins to slow down and your body does the exact opposite of what you want it to do: it hoards fat to protect itself from what it perceives as a time of famine. So you should try to snack on a healthy mix of foods every three to five hours.

MYTH #6
I don't really need to drink water!

Wrong! You should drink one ounce of water for every pound of body weight every day. That means 140 ounces of H_2O for someone that weighs 140 lbs! Water allows your body to rid itself of toxins and helps your body maintain a consistent temperature. If your body is dehydrated, it goes into maintenance mode and stores fat under the skin for insulation. Most people have trouble drinking a lot of water, but the more you drink, the more thirst you have for it, and the stronger you will become.

MYTH # 7
Oil will make my skin oily!

Wrong! The reason for oily skin is because the body is working to replace the oil missing from our diets. But you want to eat the right kind of oil. Omega-3 fats (in fish, nuts and olive oil) are known to be an important part of a healthy diet, and studies indicate that they have direct skin care and hair care benefits, giving more shine to hair and more glow to skin.

*Real Girls
MTV to You and Me

We all have those days when we feel heavier. We call them "fat days." We probably haven't gained one ounce since the day before, but there's something about the way we look in the mirror, or how our jeans fit us differently, that makes us feel fat. What do you do when you feel that way? We asked our real girls:

What do you do to feel better about yourself when you're having a "fat day?"

Elaine W.: "I cry. Crying helps me release my frustration. Better letting it out than keeping it in. Or I go dance or play volleyball.

Searcy C.: "Besides crying, I might go ahead and change my whole 'look.' But if I can't change my look, I try to have a normal day anyway."

Erica M.: "I'll do a whole bunch of stomach crunches and use the ab slide for my stomach. I'll stop looking at myself until I feel differently."

Christy G.: "When I have a 'fat day,' I just wear comfortable clothes, like jeans and a sweatshirt. I'll tell myself that I don't care what anybody else thinks. It's all mental."

Kathy W.: "I usually eat less, and try to wear clothes that are a bit more flattering."

Brittany H.: "I used to make myself throw up. I felt so empty. But since I've gotten over that, I put my energy into things like exercising and changing other parts of myself, like washing and styling my hair or painting my nails. And even though it may sound weird, shaving my legs actually makes me feel skinnier."

Macall R.: "Most of the time I don't eat as much as I would usually. It doesn't always work, so I tell myself that from now on, I'm not going to eat as much so I can lose weight. But that never happens."

Nicole R.: "When I feel fat, I try and do some stomach crunches or suck my stomach in. And I try to wear baggy clothes so you can't see my stomach."

Emily C.: "I change clothes about a thousand times."

*Real Guys
MTV to You and Me

Food. This four letter F-word causes girls to feel panicked, needy, guilty, excited— sometimes all at once. If there's a girl who has a 100% healthy attitude toward food then we have yet to meet her. So we went and asked the guys this way-out question:

If you could give girls you care about a letter that they had to read before every meal, what would it say? (They had some answers that are worth digesting.)

E.J. Y.: "You shouldn't starve yourselves. You shouldn't really worry about what guys think. When I have lunch or dinner with girls and they only order a salad, it drives me nuts."

Drew W.: "I wish you could enjoy the meal. Block out your anxieties and fears. Picture how guys eat. They chow with relentlessness and without any worries. Don't let appearance ruin your appetite."

Jonathan M.: "Don't worry so much about food. Your looks didn't attract me to you. It was your personality."

Chris J.: "I really care about you and I want you to love yourself for who you are, since that's the way I love you."

Brandon W.: "If you are hungry, eat. Your personality is a thousand times more attractive than your body."

Michael K.: "Remember that outside appearance is important, but it's not so important that you have to starve yourselves or worry that food will make you bigger. If you want to eat something, go for it."

Kevin C.: "Take care of yourself. Eat as much as you need. Eat healthy. If you feel overweight, don't hurt yourself by not eating at all. Do some exercise to make yourself even more healthy. Please take care of yourself. The effects of eating disorders are so lasting and widespread. Love doesn't have to do with weight."

The average teenager goes shopping 54 times per year. Keep in mind that there are only 52 weeks in a year.

Is it just me, or do dressing rooms make you look like dog meat too? I can be having a great Saturday afternoon at the mall with friends. We've munched on soft pretzels. We've slurped down our blended vanilla lattes. We walk into a cool store and pick out a few pairs of pants to try on, and bang. It hits us.

Why is it that dressing room lights always have those yellow-green fluorescent bulbs in them that turn your skin a kind of puke color?

And why is it that the mirrors make you look about ten pounds heavier?

Why is it that it seems like clothing stores put you in these ice-cube sized dressing rooms with poor lighting and weight-gaining mirrors when you try on clothes? Are they trying to make you feel bad about yourself so you'll buy something just to cover up the body in the mirror that embarrasses you?

Maybe. Maybe not. Maybe stores don't realize what they're doing, and how they're making you feel.

But it's about time you get the 411. The truth is that most of the time you come home from the mall, you feel worse about yourself, not better. Even if you got the jacket that you wanted, you saw all sorts of cool shoes that you couldn't afford. Even if you got that lipstick that you've been eyeing for a month, you didn't feel so pretty when you handed your money over to the gorgeous woman at the make-up counter.

We're not saying you should never set foot in a mall. What we are saying is that it's possible to walk out of the mall feeling better about yourself than when you walked in if you follow the steps below and read the articles in this chapter.

1. *Before you buy something, put it on hold.*
   Next time that you're pretty sure the black sweater is worth the $37, put it on hold at the store instead of buying it. For one thing, you might find an even better sweater three stores down. Plus, at the end of the day, if you decide it's not worth it to walk all the way down the mall to actually buy the first black sweater, it probably wasn't worth your money. You come home feeling better about the choices you've made and the clothes you've bought.

2. *Take friends along.*
   Encouraging friends, that is. Invite a few friends who have the courage to say to you, "That skirt isn't very flattering," but can do it gently. That way, when you try on a different skirt and they're telling you how cute it looks, you'll know that they mean it and aren't just telling you what they think you want to hear.

3. *Don't go when you're bummed.*
   Women of all ages (from your little sister to your great grandmother) often go shopping to cheer themselves up. Bad idea. If you have money, you're likely to buy something you'll regret, and if you don't have money, you're bound to feel worse by the time you get back to your house. Before you were just bummed. Now you're bummed and poor.

We've got some other ideas in this chapter to help you feel better about yourself when you go shopping, flip through magazines, or watch television. Try them out. They might make you feel like a million bucks without spending an extra cent.

The Therapist and the Frog

By Kendall

I know a therapist who has a folder in her office that she keeps pictures in. The pictures range from humans to nature to animals to colors, mostly pulled out of modern magazines. When her younger, less talkative clients, come to their session, she brings out the folder. She asks them to choose a picture of the day and a picture of the week. After they've made their selections she'll say something along the lines of, "hmmmmm... that's an interesting choice. (While nodding her head and furrowing her brow) Now tell me, why did you pick that one?" And with that, therapy has begun.

By listening and considering carefully their picture choices, she opens them up to talk about their feelings before they even realize they're doing it. Conversation is easier when you can talk about someone's feelings towards "something" instead of talking about their feelings about themselves.

One day a client left a *Teen People* magazine in her office. The therapist, in her mid-fifties, was not an avid Teen People reader, and decided to throw it in the trash. Then she remembered her picture folder, sat down and began to flip through the pages looking for pictures. After looking at every single page in the entire magazine, (cover to cover!), she closed it without pulling a single picture. There was nothing even remotely appropriate to put in her file.

Every shot of a woman was borderline pornographic. Either the women had cleavage hanging out of their blouse, a skirt so short you couldn't wear it in public, or pants so tight and pulled so low you could almost see pubic hair.

Every shot of a man and woman together was sexual, either in suggestion or actuality. She was shocked. For the first time in a long time she was faced with the realities that young people are faced with every day.

She remarked to me, "There is so much pressure on young girls to be sexy!" I looked back at her, momentarily stunned silent at this incredible grasp of the obvious and brilliantly replied, "no-duh!"

Next she asked me a strange question (that's what they're licensed to do. Ask strange questions with apparently no obvious meaning and arrive at an obscure conclusion that makes you cry most of the time!)

She asked, "Do you know what a frog would do if you put it into a pot of boiling water?"

"Ummm.... Jump out?" I said with a stupid, antagonizing smile on my face.

"Exactly! (She was not deterred from making her point by my inability to be serious) because it's hot and it will kill him if he stays in it. Having been just dropped into the pot he recognizes it's potential to cook him!"

"Its like his natural instinct." I added.

"Yes," she said. "But if you took that same frog, even with all his natural instinct, and put him in a pot of cold water on a stove top that was slowly heating up, he wouldn't realize the temperature was rising, and therefore would never jump out. Even when it starts to boil!"

"Bummer..." I said sounding like Keanu Reeves in "Bill and Ted's Excellent Adventure." I'll admit, it was not my finest or most poetic conversation ever.

As I thought about this sad little analogy of the boiled frog, I realized what she was trying to get me to see. Most times I'll get out of a situation immediately when I feel uncomfortable immediately. The situations that slowly heat up are the ones that burn us!

This therapist did not grow up watching Britney Spears strip tease on MTV in the morning over a bowl of CHEERIOS before heading out to school. She didn't have friends who wore their jeans so low on purpose so that guys could see their g-string underwear. She didn't have school shootings. She didn't have a 50% (or whatever it is) divorce rate. She didn't know the meaning of anorexia or bulimia. She didn't have porn websites at the touch of a button. And so she, like the first frog, looks through the *Teen People* magazine and says to herself, "Ouch! This is hot! Get out or you're gonna die!"

Our generation is like the second frog. We've been in the water as long as we can remember. It's getting hotter and we can't tell. We were born in this pot, and maybe that gives new meaning to the words of Jesus when he says, "I assure you that unless you are born again, you can never see the Kingdom of God." (John 3:3) Maybe he sees that we are immersed in a culture that is set up to destroy our self-esteem, bent on keeping us from living out God's purpose for our lives, turning our attention from committing our lives to God and living out his love to keeping up superficial appearances and envying what others have. If we stay in this heating water it will eventually, ever so slowly and without warning...kill us spiritually. Jesus offers us a new life. I never thought I could learn so much from a therapist and a frog!

The Mighty Magazine

Whether you know it or not, magazines like *Teen People* do influence the way you feel about yourself. Some people did a test to see if there was any connection between magazines and how we girls feel about ourselves. One at a time, they brought 39 different female college students into a room to wait several minutes before taking a test to see how satisfied they were with their bodies. Half of the women viewed *Vogue, Bazaar, Wile*, and *Allure* while they waited; the other half looked at news magazines like *Time, Newsweek, U.S. News and World Report*, and *Business Week*.

In top teen magazines, 35% of the articles focus on dating and 37% deal with appearance. That leaves just 28% for everything else.

(Liz Stevens, "Today's Teen Magazines May Be Sending Mixed Messages to Girls," Knight-Ridder/Tribute News Service, 1999.)

The women who viewed the fashion magazines ended up more bummed about how they looked. They wished they weighed less, were more frustrated about their weight, were more preoccupied with the desire to be thin, and were more afraid of getting fat than the other half of the women who looked at news magazines. And get this, there was no significant differences between the weights and heights of the two groups. The major difference was in the type of magazine they flipped through before taking the test.

Think about it...

* Does your own experience support the results of this study? Why?

* Given this, what changes, if any, should you make in the magazines you look through?

JUST A MAGAZINE

Seventeen magazine is the most popular magazine for teenage girls. It has a circulation of over 2.5 million. But others are catching up. *YM* sells 2.2 million copies and *Teen People* sells 1.6 million copies per year. These magazines are everywhere; they're in girls' lockers, backpacks, and bathrooms.

The more girls these magazines reach, the more controversy they raise. Some people fault *Seventeen* magazine for being too focused on girls' looks instead of dreams. Others criticize it for focusing more on how girls feel than how girls think.

But me, I look forward to it. I read it the night I get it in the mail, at least the first half of it. I save the second half for the next night. I read almost every article, but what I really like are the advertisements. How would I know how to do my eyeliner and what shoes are hip without them?

I wish people would stop criticizing it and just appreciate it for what it is.

Think about it...

* Can you relate to how this girl feels? Why?

* What do you learn from Seventeen and other magazines?

* Do you think it affects how you feel about yourself? If so, how?

The Haircut:
The Key to Feeling Beautiful

A haircut is supposed to make you feel better about yourself, isn't it? You spend all this money and time sitting in that chair, and you're supposed to walk out of the salon feeling more beautiful. Right?

That's not how it works for me. First off, the woman who cuts my hair could be a model. She's gorgeous. I see the guys in the salon staring at her. Sure, they try not to be obvious, but since I'm sitting in front of the mirror, I can see what they're doing. Their eyes barely glance in my direction. They stay glued to my hairdresser.

Plus there's all that time staring at the mirror. A big mirror. A well-lit mirror. The nose that is too chubby and the eyes that are too far apart are there staring at me. I can't run away quickly like I normally do when I'm doing my make-up in the morning. It's my very own special 45 minute date with the mirror.

And I never come out as good as I think I'm going to. I walk in thinking to myself, "Great, this is going to do the trick. No more plain Jane anymore." But even though I leave with less split ends and the haircut all the movie stars have, it's still pretty much the same ol' me.

Get this: even if I do leave looking pretty good, by the next morning, my perfect hair is just a big mountain of bed head. And even though I spend 20 minutes drying and curling my hair, it never looks as good when I do it myself.

Bottom line: It costs me 45 minutes and $37. And what do I get out of it? A dose of disappointment big enough to choke on.

Think about it...

* How do you feel when you get your haircut? Why?

* Do you leave feeling better, worse, or the same about yourself as when you walked in? Why?

* Two days later, how do you feel about yourself?

* So should you change how frequently you get your haircut—like rarely get it cut, or get it cut more often? Why?

* What's the purpose of a haircut, anyway? Is it about the health of your hair and how much of it is about the way you look? Why?

The Secret Vomit

When I throw up, I like to use a bag instead of the toilet. That way I can seal up the bag and throw it in my backpack.

Sometimes when I'm walking from class to class, I stop in the hallway and pull out the bag. It's a squishy, beautiful combination of orange, yellow, and green. Mm-mm.

When I'm by myself, I like to smell it. Brings back fond memories. Banana pudding. Yum.

No one knows what I do. It's just my little secret.

OK, is it just me, or are you a little queasy right now?

Saving your vomit and returning to it over and over again is pretty gross. Believe it or not, the Bible actually relates to this person.

The writer of Proverbs 26:11 warns, "As a dog returns to its vomit, so a fool repeats his folly."

Yuck. God sure doesn't mince words.

Someone who makes the same mistake over and over again is no different than someone who goes back to their vomit.

So how does this relate to you?

Do this: Circle anything on this list that makes you feel bad about yourself.

Magazine covers

Magazine ads about make-up

Magazine ads about hair

Magazine articles about dieting

Clothing catalogsl

Shows about famous celebrities (like "Extra," "Access Hollywood," and " Entertainment Tonight")

TV ads for Victoria's Secret

TV ads for gyms

The news

Soap operas

Game shows

Mannequins in store windows

Trying on clothes

Your favorite TV show

TV shows about kids your age

Movies about kids your age

Music videos and/or MTV

Other _____

Do this: Now rank your top 5. Write 1 beside the thing that makes you feel the worst about yourself, then 2, etc., down to 5.

Whatever you ranked, if you keep going back to something that makes you feel worse, you're just like that dog, tramping its feet in that smelly puke. Almost makes you want to change, doesn't it?

Think about it:

* How does watching MTV make you feel about yourself?

* What is the answer for keeping your self-image healthy—not reading magazines, watching MTV, and staying away from the mall? Explain.

* What are the magazines, shows, books, catalogs, websites, etc. that cause you to feel better about yourself? Explain.

Romancing Yourself

How do you define "romance"? In your mind does it always conjure up images of a boy and a girl? Do you need a guy in your life to have romance? Well, the *Oxford Dictionary* defines romance as an "atmosphere or tendency characterized by a sense of remoteness from or idealization of every day life." It defines romantic, "as of, or characterized by…an idealized, sentimental, or fantastic view of reality."

What this should tell you is that every minute of your solitude can be romantic; you don't need to have a boyfriend. Romance is an atmosphere you can live in. It is not the silly sentimentality that most young lovers try to pursue by holding hands or writing little poems or calling each other pet names. It transcends such barriers as physical distance. You can sit alone and gaze at a sunset and feel a deep sense of romance. Most of the time, sharing it only dilutes its power anyway when your partner doesn't regard it with the same respect.

Of course we all long for the day when the second part of the definition comes to fruition. "A prevailing sense of wonder or mystery surrounding the mutual attraction in a love affair." Finally free to combine the romance of our lives with the romance of his. But if you're not there yet, then don't pretend to be! Live in the now.

Look inside yourself and to God for the fulfillment of all of your longings. And be confident that the desire for romance is natural, even more than that; it is wonderful! Only when you learn to find it from within will you feel satisfied when it comes externally.

And so I have compiled my top 10 most romantic things to do by yourself! I do all of these as often as I can. At first it's a little strange, and you think people are staring at you wondering why you're all alone. But that feeling passes eventually. I hope that if you choose to do them, you will do so with a deep sense of love for yourself! Because in the words of Rainer Maria Rilke, "What goes on in your innermost being is worthy of your whole love."

Did You KNOW...

People magazine polled 1,000 women, ages 18-35. Poll results indicated that the portrayal of women on television and in the movies makes 37% of women feel insecure about their bodies. One woman explained that when she sees pictures of Julia Roberts, she tries to look only at her eyes and not her body because Roberts' figure makes her feel like a "slob."

(Julie K.L. Dam, "How Do I Look?" People, September 4, 2000, 114-118.)

In the island of Fiji, women used to want to be plump because that meant they had enough food to eat. Three years after television and western cultural values arrived on the island, the number of teen girls who had inducted vomiting to control weight jumped from 3% to 15%. Eating disorders more than doubled. Those who watched television at least three times per week were 50% more likely than other girls to see themselves as fat, even though their actual weights were the same as the other girls.

(Kim A. McDonald, "Eating Disorders Rise with Arrival of TV," *The Chronicle of Higher Education*, June 11, 1999.)

By the year 2010, teen girls will swell from 31 million to 35 million in America. Adolescent girls spend $60 billion annually.

(Jancee Dunn, "The Secret Life of Teenage Girls," *Rolling Stone*, November 11, 1999.)

✳ The Top 10 Most Romantic
Things to do by Yourself

10. Bake yourself some cookies.
(I mean your favorite cookies.) Decorate a shoebox and line it with tin foil. Put all your cookies inside and hide them in your room so that no one can find them. Or go to your local candy store and pick all your absolute favorite chocolates. Eat them all yourself!

9. Take a bubble bath!
Take a long indulgent soak in some smell-good suds. I always put more than the directions tell me to! If it says pour one capful into running water, I put three! If you're allowed to shave your legs, do that! Or get some cucumber slices, put them over your eyes and relax!

8. Go on a hike or prayer walk at sunrise or sunset.
Around my house, I have a trail that leads back about a mile to a waterfall. I love to get a backpack with water and snacks and hike to it. Or sometimes I'll set out with a friend or by myself and just pray the whole walk. When I try to sit at home and pray I normally get fidgety and can't concentrate. This way I can be moving and yet still fully concentrating on God. Sunrise is a hard one for me, but I never regret doing it! Sunset is always stunning!

7. Plan a picnic in the park.
And take your dog! If you don't have a dog, borrow one from a neighbor. Get yourself a big wicker basket and pack a sandwich, drink, dessert and a big blanket to sit on (preferably red and white checkered, it just looks cuter) and go outside! We spend so much of our life indoors looking at man made inventions like TV or the Internet. There is so much beauty outside, so take a good look around! Eat very slowly. Enjoy each bite!

6. Fire in the fireplace with a good book.
Lay some pillows from your couch or your bed down in front of the fireplace. Prop yourself up so you can see, and read by the light of the fire. The three-hour Duraflame logs are perfect for this. If you finish your book just enjoy the fire.

5. Pick yourself a bunch of flowers.
(Not the one's your mom has planted in the back yard! Go find some wild ones.) Get a vase and fill your room with them. Take special time to smell each one and thank God that he created it! Think of it as God giving you flowers!

4. Have a matinee and ice cream day.
Save your money for a Saturday afternoon and go see a movie BY YOURSELF! Most people can't do that. I absolutely love going to movies alone. Then treat yourself to an extra large ice cream cone. Take a walk and eat it remembering your favorite parts of the movie.

3. Hit the bookstore, plus coffee.
Hopefully you have a Barnes and Noble or Borders bookstore around you somewhere. Get yourself a hot drink; find a book that interests you and a big cozy chair. Spend a few hours reading. You don't have to finish it. Or you could just get five or six magazines and look through them. (One of my guiltiest pleasures is thumbing through *Brides* magazines. That normally freaks guys out, but if you're alone it doesn't matter!!)

2. Make yourself a gourmet dinner.
You might have to save your money for this one… Look through a cookbook or go on the Internet and find recipes for an appetizer, main course, and dessert. (Not macaroni and cheese!) Try something you've never made before! (That's the fun of it!) Go to the grocery store and get all the necessary ingredients and test your culinary skills. Then set your place at the table very fancy using a tablecloth, light a candle and put on some beautiful music. *Bon Appétite!*

1. Take a walk in the rain (umbrella optional).
The next time it rains, go outside and walk in it. Take a long stroll! Enjoy it, catch some drops in your mouth and jump in some puddles. Sing your favorite song under your breath or at the top of your lungs (if you feel so brave and providing no one can hear you!)

Real Girls
MTV to You and Me

MTV not only reflects youth culture, it shapes it. But does it shape how we feel about ourselves? Maybe even more interestingly, does it have different effects on guys and girls? We asked our real girls and guys how MTV made them feel about themselves. We'll start with the real girls' answers. After all, ladies first.

Kathy W.: "It makes me feel worse. I start comparing myself to all the 'hot' and skinny girls."

Nicole R.: "When I watch MTV, I feel glad that I have God because celebrities that I see seem kinda lost, so I wouldn't want to be them."

Emily B.: "I really don't watch MTV much, but some of the videos really disgust me. Especially when guys drool over the women on them."

Searcy C.: "MTV makes me feel ugly, fat, and unwanted. The girls on there are like size 2 with huge chests. I feel like I could never reach their standards."

Brittany H.: "It makes me feel way worse about myself. I can't eat while I watch it because I gross myself out. I see what they have and I want that."

Elaine W.: "It makes me feel ugly. To see all those skinny, pretty girls makes my confidence go way down."

Christy G.: "I rarely watch it, but when I do, it seems like a whole bunch of 'perfect' people. I don't fit those categories."

Macall R.: "When I watch MTV, I feel like I'm never skinny enough."

Erica M.: "On the one hand, the people seem successful so it makes me want to try harder. On the other hand, it discourages me because my body doesn't look like theirs."

Real Guys
MTV to You and Me

Let's turn to the guys. As you read what they write about how MTV makes them feel about themselves, try to figure out if it's different from what the ladies have already said.

Jonathan: "I'm just watching for entertainment. It doesn't change how I feel about myself."

Drew W.: "Appearance-wise, it makes me feel inferior because all the stars are good looking. But it doesn't phase me much."

Kevin C.: "It doesn't really affect how I feel about myself, but it does affect my lifestyle. It makes me wish I had more money, or that particular car."

Brandon: "It doesn't really have an effect on me."

E.J. Y.: "I really don't think it has any effect on me."

Think About it...

* So what differences do you notice between how the real girls and real guys answered?

* Similarities? Differences? Why do you think that is? Is it about what's on MTV? How girls and guys are different? Both?

* How does MTV make you feel about yourself? Why?